W9-ABS-063

Commercial Fishing Methods

Commercial Fishing Methods

—an introduction to vessels and gears

John C. Sainsbury

Fishing News (Books) Ltd
23 Rosemount Avenue, West Byfleet, Surrey

First printed in 1971
Reprinted 1975

Printed by The Whitefriars Press Ltd.
London and Tonbridge

Contents

List of Figures

Foreword

THIS book was first written as a text for use in the training of potential commercial fishermen at the University of Rhode Island in the United States. It was prepared to provide an introduction to the important commercial fishing methods of the world together with the vessels and gear used in them.

Many volumes can be written about each fishing method and it has not been possible, in this book, to do more than describe the operation and equipment in general terms; many variations in rigging of vessels and gear are found in practice and readers are referred to the list of further reading which has been included.

In addition to students it is hoped that the material will be of use to the many scientists, engineers, economists and other people who are beginning work with the commercial fishing industry and need to have some knowledge of the manner in which fishing is carried out.

I am greatly indebted to the following for many of the illustrations: Marine Construction and Design Co., Seattle; National Fisherman, Camden, Maine; World Fishing, London; Fishing News International, London; Canadian Fisherman, Montreal; U.S. National Marine Fisheries Service, Washington; David Thomson, Scotland.

Mr. Joseph Austin, photographer, College of Resource Development, University of Rhode Island has been of immense assistance in preparing the illustrations.

John Sainsbury
Narragansett, Rhode Island

Introduction

FOR many thousands of years, living creatures of the sea have provided man with one of his principal sources of food. This is true today, and food from the sea continues to grow in importance as efforts are made to establish sufficient resources to feed the multiplying world population, production being unable to keep up with growing demands for protein.

Many years ago man made the change from hunting to farming animals, so achieving a much greater supply of food than was possible from hunting the natural wild stocks. This sophistication has not yet been achieved so far as sea life is concerned, although encouraging results are being achieved with several species of fish, and commercial farming of both freshwater fish and some shellfish is a successful reality in a number of countries. The bulk of the world's sea food supply continues to come from the stocks of ocean fish and other sea creatures, whose boundaries of movement are governed by natural characteristics of individual species and the ocean environment.

As the naturally occurring ocean stocks of fish are not yet fully utilized, commercial fishermen are hunters and likely to remain so for the foreseeable future. While fish farming will grow rapidly in importance, it would appear that there will be a place for the commercial fisherman for a great many years in the future.

To many eyes the methods and equipment used by fishermen appear crude and unsophisticated; in fact, so far as modern commercial fishing is concerned, the opposite is true in most of the world's important fisheries. Technology, sophistication, complexity and investment in vessels and equipment, together with techniques of finding and bringing fish to port, are showing rapid growth. Increasing investment in research and development is continually improving the efficiency of operation and conditions under which fishermen work.

In order for a fishing operation to be successful, it must be economically viable within the structure in which it operates; if a fisherman does not achieve sufficient financial reward, then he cannot continue fishing. Any technological development that does not more than pay for itself is unlikely to be of benefit to the fisherman or to be used by him.

Many different methods of fishing and types of fishing gear for catching commercially important sea life have emerged over the centuries; their continued use and development to meet local conditions in many parts of the world has led to the sophistication of today's operation.

The last two decades have seen new concepts introduced, an increased application of technology and accelerated development of existing methods. Continuing development is enabling methods that have stood the test of time to be used in the harvesting of hitherto unutilized stocks of the world's oceans.

Choice of Fishing Method and Gear

Many factors enter into the choice of the method and gear used to catch a particular species in a particular area. Principally, the choice will depend on:
1. The species being fished
2. Individual value of the species to the fisherman
3. The depth of water
4. The characteristics of the sea bed, if gear is to be worked in contact with the bottom.

Species Being Fished

The various species of commercially important sea life (see Fig. 1) have differing habits, movements, and reactions to stimuli; shellfish, such as lobster, crab, scallops, clams, and oysters, are found living on or in the sea bed. Some species of fish, such as cod and haddock, are often found near the sea bed, while flounder and other flatfish will often be lying on or just beneath the bottom if it is sandy; these demersal species, or groundfish, are usually caught by fishing gear worked on the sea bed, as are the shellfish mentioned above.

Pelagic species, such as herring, tuna, capelin and swordfish, may be found anywhere between the sea bed and the surface, and these are normally taken by fishing gear that is not in contact with the bottom; in certain circumstances, as with herring while spawning, the fish tend to congregate in shallow water and may be caught by various types of fishing gear worked on the sea bed.

The movements and habits of each species are controlled by such factors as water temperature, salinity, spawning habits, migration, available food resources, and in many cases, particularly as far as pelagic species are concerned, by the thermoclines

Fig. 1. Classification of fish for harvesting. The species here are only a selection of those important in each group as food or material.

or temperature barriers that exist in any particular location.

Some fish, such as herring, tuna, and anchovy, congregate in dense schools so that they can be taken in bulk; other species, such as lobster and many demersal fish, are more loosely distributed, and yet others will often be found singly or in small scattered groups.

Individual Value

Depending on the way in which it is processed and marketed, a certain type of fish may have a high, medium, or low individual value; the worth of the same species varies considerably in different parts of the world in accord with local traditions, habits and preferences.

Examples of high individual value are salmon, lobsters, oysters, scallops, tuna, swordfish, while at the opposite end of the scale and of low individual value are fish used primarily for reduction into animal feeds, such as pet foods or fish meal.

Species marketed as fresh or frozen "food fish" (fish consumed for its own sake with a minimum of processing, such as haddock or sole) normally come into the medium value bracket, but when used as a basis for fish fingers or portions their individual value is lowered.

Wide variations in individual value may appear; such is the case with herring, which is used primarily as a bulk fish for reduction into meal, but brings a far higher individual value when processed into "kippers". Similarly, the anchovy is the mainstay of the Peruvian fish meal industry with a very low individual value, but when canned becomes a delicacy of high value.

The type of fishing gear used must also take into account the use and value of the individual fish, for instance, both salmon and mackerel can be taken by trolling with a hook and line; this is a viable means in the case of the large salmon of high individual value, but would be ridiculous gear to use in order to catch mackerel for bulk processing into meal.

Also bound up with the use and value of fish is the quality required; this may be affected considerably by the type of fishing gear used—one particular type of gear may mutilate some portion of the catch during the operation, while other gear may deliver the catch in prime condition.

Depth of Water

The various types of fishing gear are designed to be operated within particular depths of water,

typically: in the surface region of deep oceans, on the sea bed of the continental shelves or shallow regions, or between surface and bottom where depth is not too great. Depth of water will therefore exert considerable influence on the choice of suitable gear.

Characteristics of Sea Bed

Some types of fishing gear, particularly those which rely for effectiveness on their movement over the bottom, are susceptible to damage from hard, uneven or rough sea beds, and it is often impossible to use them due to the bottom topography being unsuitable. In many cases static gear can be placed on the sea bed with little problem.

Economic Considerations

In addition to the technical factors, economic considerations are of prime importance. It must be possible, using the particular method selected, to catch and bring to market sufficient quantities of fish to provide a viable operation economically. If several techniques appear technically acceptable, the one estimated to provide greatest economic return is the usual choice.

Principal Types of Gear

The principal types of fishing gear in use by fishing vessels are shown diagrammatically in Figure 2. In some cases the gear will be towed by the vessel, in some it will be used to encircle a school of fish, while in others the gear is static, being left in one place for a while and then retrieved together with its catch.

Several methods of fishing utilize gear which can be operated anywhere from the sea bed to the surface, i.e., in "mid-water"; in other methods, use of the gear is restricted by its design and present techniques of operation to near the surface, or on the sea bed. An idea of the manner of use and depth of water in which the various types of fishing gear are commonly used may be gained from Figure 2.

It is convenient to group the fishing methods according to the demands they place on the operating vessel.

Towed or Dragged Gear

1. Trawling bottom otter trawling and pair trawling
2. Multi-rig bottom trawling
3. Mid-water trawling, single and pair
4. Dredging.

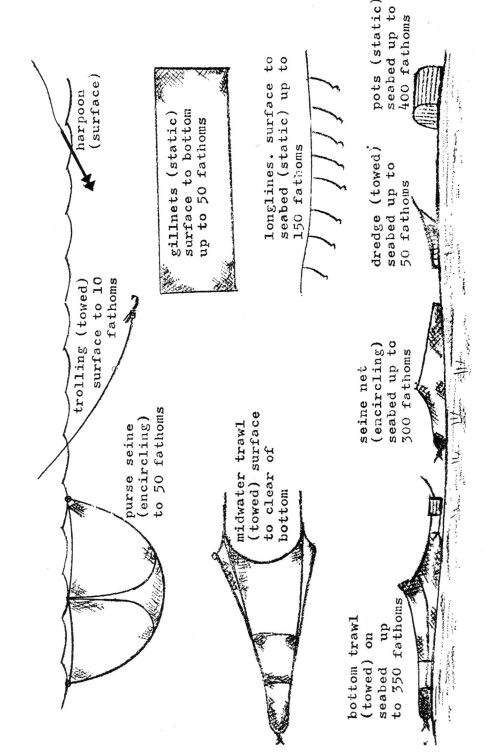

harpoon (surface)

gillnets (static) surface to bottom up to 50 fathoms

longlines. surface to seabed (static) up to 150 fathoms

pots (static) seabed up to 400 fathoms

trolling (towed) surface to 10 fathoms

purse seine (encircling) to 50 fathoms

seine net (encircling) seabed up to 300 fathoms

dredge (towed) seabed up to 50 fathoms

midwater trawl (towed) surface to clear of bottom

bottom trawl (towed) on seabed up to 350 fathoms

Fig. 2. Principal types of fishing gear.

Encircling Gear

1. Purse seining
2. Seine netting (Danish or Scottish seine).

Static Gear

1. Gillnets and setnets including traps
2. Longlining
3. Pots.

Other Mobile Gear

1. Trolling
2. Harpooning
3. Pole and line.

World wide, the most important commercially used methods are purse seining, together with its many variations, and trawling.

Purse seining is used primarily to supply raw material for reduction into animal feed stuff and fertilizer, it being a method ideally suited to capturing and handling huge quantities of fish where quality is relatively unimportant. Typical here are the menhaden and herring fisheries of the United States and Canadian East Coast, the Norwegian and Icelandic herring and capelin fisheries or Peru's anchovy fishery which keeps that country in the forefront of fish meal production.

To a lesser extent, purse seining is used, with more stringent handling and storage techniques, in the production of pilchards, various herring delicacies and tuna seen on the world's dinner tables.

Trawling provides the major part of the world's supply of fish for use directly as human food, where quality is of prime importance, the bottom fisheries of the continental shelf areas for such species as haddock, cod and shrimp being typical.

At the same time, trawling, either on bottom or in mid water, is used to capture herring and other fish for reduction purposes.

Although purse seining and trawling provide most of the world's tonnage, each of the other methods described in the following pages is of considerable importance in particular segments of the industry and in different parts of the world. For instance, the economically important king crab fishery of Alaska and the queen crab fishery of the North West Atlantic are dependent on offshore pot fishing techniques and most of the inshore crab and lobster stocks are worked with smaller pots and vessels. Again, whereas much tuna is taken by large purse seiners, longlining is of importance, especially in the Japanese industry, and pole fishing for this species using smaller vessels is common in other areas such as Australia.

Many fishing vessels have the capability of changing quickly from the use of one fishing method to another; these "combination vessels" are of particular importance in fisheries where different species are harvested, requiring different techniques, at various seasons during the year. Typical here are the combination vessels of the North Pacific Coast of Canada and the U.S.A. which convert rapidly between purse seining, trawling or longlining. Other examples may be found in the Icelandic and Norwegian purse seiners which convert to longlining, or the typical British Isles inshore vessels which trawl and use the seine net, or perhaps the ring net.

Towed or Dragged Gear

BOTTOM OTTER TRAWLING

THE trawl net is basically a large bag made of netting which is drawn along the sea bed to scoop up fish on or near the bottom. Depending on the manner in which the gear is constructed and rigged, its operating characteristics can be altered to permit use on various types of bottom and for many species of fish.

Figure 3 shows the operation, and Figure 4 the trawl in more detail. It can be seen as a large bag-shaped net, wide at one end, the mouth, which is open, leading to the body of the net which tapers to the closed end where the fish that enter through the mouth are trapped in the "cod-end".

The mouth takes up somewhat of an oval shape when viewed from the front, and two wings stretch out in front on either side to increase the area swept and to guide fish in the net's path down to the cod-end. Around the upper edge of the mouth runs the "headline" to which are fixed a number of floats, and around the bottom of the mouth is the ground rope which is in contact with the bottom and is weighted. The combined effect of the floats on the headline and the weighted groundline keeps the mouth open vertically.

The ground rope may be weighted with chain, or it may be merely wire when the net is being operated on a clear bottom; when used on rough bottom, iron or rubber rollers are rigged to assist its passage (see Fig. 5).

As may be seen from Figure 3, the headline and top of the mouth usually overhang the footrope and bottom of the mouth to ensure that fish disturbed by the groundrope do not swim upward and escape, but are shepherded down into the cod-end.

The Otter Boards

Horizontal spread of the mouth is attained by the "otter boards" or "doors" towed ahead of the net and set at an angle of attack to the towing direction, so providing the outward force necessary to spread the wings to which they are fastened. The boards may be connected directly to the wings or separated from them by a length of wire known as the "ground cable" or "sweep line". In the latter case the sweeplines are connected to the door by a backstrap and to the net by a bridle or "dan leno" arrangement as shown in Figure 4. Actual arrangement of the connection between the backstrap and sweeplines varies, depending on the handling arrangements aboard the operating vessel, and will be described further as the various vessel layouts are considered.

The common otter board is a rectangular wood and steel structure, and is illustrated in Figure 6. The two wires forming the backstrap to the ground cable are fastened to the upper and lower corners at the outer face of the rear edge. Towing brackets are fitted to the inner face of the board to provide a towing point some two-fifths of the length from the leading edge. From the towing point, the steel warps lead up to the towing vessel.

Other types of otter board are used, such as "oval" or "V" doors, which have been designed to give greater efficiency under various circumstances (see Fig. 6).

The Cod-End

The cod-end is a funnel of netting closed at the rear end by a rope looped through the meshes or rings and tied with a special cod-end knot which is easily released. At about midlength is the "splitting

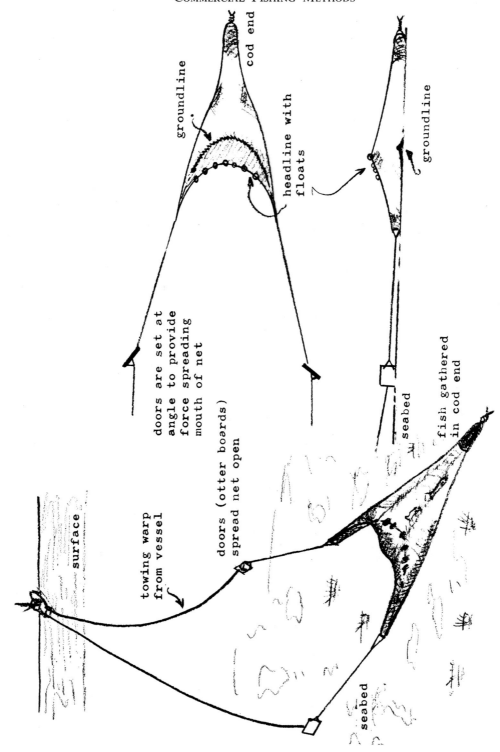

groundline

cod end

headline with floats

groundline

doors are set at angle to provide force spreading mouth of net

doors (otter boards) spread net open

towing warp from vessel

surface

seabed

fish gathered in cod end

seabed

Fig. 3. The bottom trawl.

strap", an endless length of rope running through metal rings fastened to the outside of the net, so that when it is pulled tight the net is bunched together at this point. Attached to the splitting strap a rope, known as the "bullrope" or "pork line", is run loosely along the length of the net and tied to the headline; the manner in which this rope is used in working the net will be detailed later.

Operation of Trawl Gear

The speed at which the trawl is towed over the bottom varies, depending on the species being sought, from about 1½ to 2 knots up to 4½ to 5 knots for fast swimming fish. Both vessel and gear must be designed and arranged to suit the species being caught, and wide variations in the size and rigging of the net and doors may be used to provide the correct combination and maintain the desired net geometry. Towing a particular trawl too slowly may cause the otter boards to close together, so providing insufficient spreading power to the net which tends to sag on to the bottom. On the other hand, towing too fast could result in the net lifting off the bottom and "floating", quite possibly leading to its turning over, and a "foul gear".

The size of trawls operated by small fishing vessels depends on the engine power and towing pull available, the design and construction of the gear, the

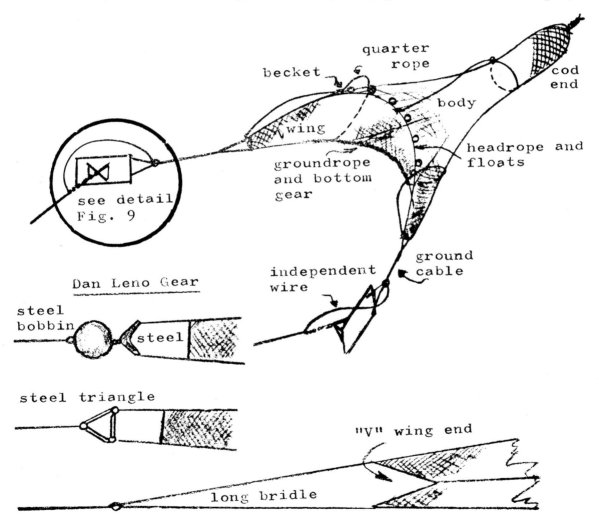

Fig. 4. The otter trawl.

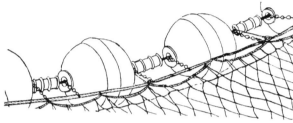

Fig. 5. Trawl bottom gear: other types of bottom gear, having lighter construction, are shown in Figures 20 and 24.
Top: heavy gear around the coaming of a large stern ramp trawler.
Bottom: heavy steel bobbins are spaced along and connected to the footrope.

vessel's size, and the handling space and arrangements aboard.

Generally, the size as it affects the design of vessels in terms of layout, space, and equipment may be discussed in terms of the headline length, the mesh and twine size, the number of meshes round the mouth, and the length, together with the type and weight of such items as the bottom gear, and in particular the doors, which can account for some third of the total drag.

When at the fishing grounds, the trawling operation is a continuous sequence of setting out the gear from aboard, towing the net (usually for between one and three hours), and then hauling back the net, emptying the catch from the cod-end, and setting out again for the next tow.

Two distinct vessel layouts are in general use— the side trawler in which the net is set and retrieved over the side, and the stern trawler in which the operation takes place over the stern.

The last decade has seen a gradual acceptance of the principles of stern trawling, and the number of side trawlers built each year is decreasing as the number of small stern trawlers put into service increases. A study of fishing vessel completions during the period 1965 to 1970 shows that a large number of side trawlers are still being delivered, so that a description of their operation is included. Certainly for a "combination vessel" using two or more methods of fishing during the year, side trawling may be an important factor.

Fig. 6. Common types of otter board or door; each type can vary in design and construction depending on its purpose and local practice.
Left: standard rectangular otter board (wood).   Middle: 'V' type otter board (steel).   Right: oval otter board (wood).

SIDE TRAWLING

Figures 7 to 12 clearly illustrate the operation of traditional small side trawlers, and an outline typical arrangement of the vessels. They are of a single deck design, usually having a forecastle which is often of a whaleback construction, and the wheelhouse aft with the engine room below. The working deck is forward with one or more hatches to the holds below. Crew accommodation on most modern vessels is aft, at and below the wheelhouse level, but in older vessels use is made of the forecastle.

Forward of the wheelhouse is the winch, usually with two main barrels on which the towing warps are wound, and two warping heads or gypsies for handling running lines. The position of the winch varies considerably, and it may be placed anywhere on the foredeck to allow convenient runs of the

working wires (Fig. 8 shows one example of the arrangement and Fig. 14 another).

The gallows, massive well-braced steel structures, which take the towing pull of the warps, are situated one just abaft the forecastle, and the other abreast the wheelhouse. A well-stayed mast is sited at the forward end of the working deck, and in some designs a second mast is sited aft.

The arrangement of other important items of equipment for working the gear will be detailed as the operation of the gear is described.

Arrangement of Trawl Gear for Side Trawling

The towing warps from the vessel end in a short length of chain that is connected to the towing brackets on the doors by a flat link/G-link combination so that it may be easily engaged and disengaged.

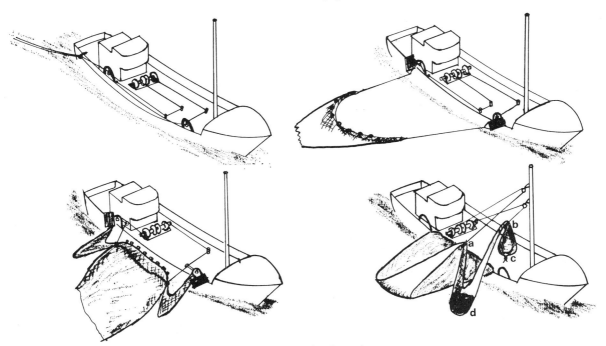

Fig. 7. Side Trawler Operation.

Top left: when towing, the warps pass from the winch drums over the deck bollards forward to sheaves at the base of gallows and over the gallows blocks. They are clamped together in the towing block.

Top Right: first stage in hauling. The winch has heaved in the warps until doors are at gallows where they are hooked up on dog chain. Doors are then released from warps and winch heaves wings to gallows, the ground cable running freely through the Kelly's eye.

Bottom left: heaving in the mouth. Once wings are at the gallows, quarter ropes are untied and taken to warping drums to pull mouth together and above the rail.

Bottom right: heaving in the bag. The splitting operation is shown where whip and falls are used to bring a large catch aboard, one bag at a time.

Of particular importance in taking aboard and setting the net on a side trawler is the connection between doors and the ground cables. Figures 4 and 9 show this; the backstrap on each door ends in a steel ring known as the "Kelly's eye". The end of the ground cable passes through the Kelly's eye and is connected to a "keep" or "stopper"; the end of the stopper connected to the ground cable is small enough to fit into the eye, but it then widens sharply so that it jams into the eye and transmits the pull from the door to the ground cable (see Fig. 9). The section of the stopper that is forward of the eye is fastened to a wire or chain, known as the "independent wire", which is of a length to lie loosely around the door with its other end secured to the chain that terminates the towing warps.

Quarter ropes are fitted to the trawl net (see Fig. 4). These are connected to the groundrope, one each side, roughly at the point where the wings merge into the body of the net. They then pass round the outside of the net and through rings attached to the headline, and so to the wings where they are fastened temporarily. These ropes are used in bringing the net aboard the vessel, and it is important that they run loosely through the rings on the headline.

Towing Arrangements Aboard the Vessel

Using the deck arrangement of Figure 7, the towing warps are wound on to the two drums of the trawl winch. The port (forward) warp is run forward round a deck bollard through a sheave at

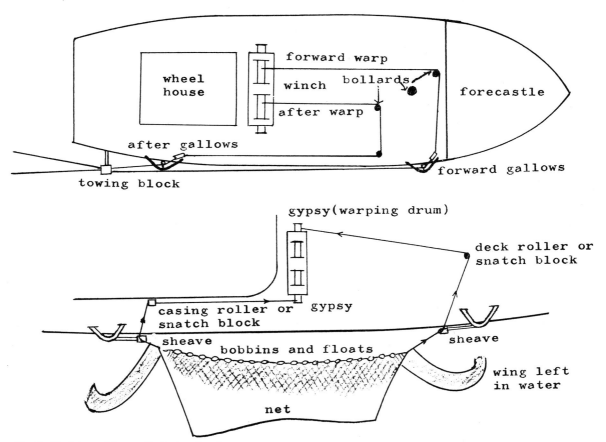

Fig. 8. Deck layout for small side trawler. A very common arrangement, and the one used when describing the side trawler operation. Quarter rope sheaves mounted on framework from gallows, but may be mounted on posts or booms if distance between gallows is too great to permit arrangement shown.
Top: run of warps while towing.
Bottom: arrangement of sheaves and snatch blocks for quarter rope handling.

the base of the forward gallows and through the towing sheave hanging from the top of the gallows; from here the warp runs to the starboard otter board.

The warp from the starboard drum (after warp) runs forward around a deck bollard to a further bollard near the bulwark and then aft, through a sheave at the base of the after gallows and so over the after gallows sheave to the port otter board.

To ensure a common towing point and hence stability of the net while towing, the forward and after warps are caught together in a towing block abaft the after gallows.

Hauling the Gear (See Figs. 7 and 10)

When the time comes to haul up the trawl gear, both warps are released from the towing block and hauled in evenly by the winch until the doors reach the gallows (Fig. 7). The winch is then stopped and the doors hooked to the gallows by means of "dog chains" fixed to each gallows for the purpose. During this time the vessel has been slowed or stopped and turned across the wind with the working side to windward, so that the vessel is blown off the gear, to prevent fouling, and to simplify getting the net aboard over the side.

The warps are disconnected from the doors and the winch again hauls up on the warps. Now, the independent cables pull the stopper out of the Kelly's eye, and the ground cables run freely through the latter until the wings reach the gallows sheave (see Fig. 10). At this point hauling is stopped and the winch braked, securing the net in this position.

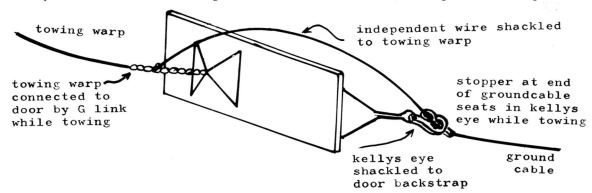

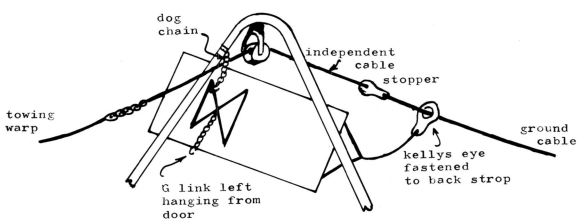

Fig. 9. Operation of Kelly's eye and stopper.

Top: while towing, the stopper jams in the Kelly's eye, transmitting the pull from doors to ground cable. The independent wire lies loosely over door.

Bottom: when hauling, doors are pulled up and hooked to gallows. Warp is disconnected from doors at G link so that strain is taken by independent wire. Hauling is continued, the stopper being pulled out of the Kelly's eye, with the ground cable passing easily through until the wings reach the gallows or the net is stretched at the rail.

Fig. 10. Side trawler hauling operation.

Top left: warps have been heaved in by winch and doors hooked up. Warps have been disconnected and winch now pulls stopper (seen below door) out of Kelly's eye. Chain forming independent wire is seen over door.

Middle: ground cable runs freely through the Kelly's eye as wings are brought up to gallows. After gallows shown.

Right: forward wing at the gallows. The quarter ropes are now untied from the wings and taken over the sheaves at "x" and "y".

Bottom left: quarter ropes are taken to warping drums. Here the forward rope is being pulled in on the port drum.

Middle: the quarters pull the mouth of the net together and heaves it up to the sheaves.

Right: the quarters are hooked up by slip hooks. The groundrope and headline are brought aboard and twine heaved in by hand.

Fig. 10 (cont'd).
Left: the bullrope is unfastened from the headline and taken over the forward quarter rope sheave to the port warping drum.
Middle: falls from overhead are hooked to the splitting strap and taken to the warping drum.
Right: the cod end is taken aboard and the fish dumped into the deck pound.

The next stage of the operation is to bring the net aboard the vessel, and this is begun by use of the quarter ropes. To handle these ropes, two sheaves are sited between the gallows, normally some 24 feet apart and some 3 feet above the rail level (see Fig. 7).

The quarter ropes are unfastened from the bridles, passed through these sheaves, and through conveniently located blocks on the working deck, to the warping drums on the winch. The after quarter rope is taken to the starboard warping head and the forward rope to the port warping head. These are heaved in together, and as they run smoothly through the rings on the headline, pull up the groundrope and bring in the mouth of the net. As the pull is continued, the headrope and footrope are brought above the rail and hooked up securely at each quarter rope sheave. The mouth of the net is brought inboard by the crew with assistance from a whip if heavy ground gear is being used, and the twine from the body of the net is pulled aboard. The bullrope is untied from the headline and taken over the forward quarter rope sheave to bring the cod-end alongside just abaft the forward gallows. When the splitting strap lies within reach, a tackle from the mast is hooked to it and taken to a whipping drum, the cod-end hoisted aboard, and the cod-end knot released allowing the catch to spill out.

Often there will be too much fish in the net to allow all to be brought aboard in one pull as described above. In that case, the operation is shown in Figure 7 where a second whip from the mast is used. First, a strap is put round the net some distance forward of the cod-end (a) and the net hauled up by one tackle; the splitting strap is handled by the second tackle (b) and hauled up so that part of the catch is brought aboard (c) and part left over the side (d). When the fish in the cod-end have been dumped, the knot is retied and the cod-end returned overboard. Now the tackle (a) is hoisted shaking the fish left in the water down into the cod-end, where it may be lifted aboard by tackle (b) and dumped. If a very large amount of fish is in the net, this operation known as "splitting" may be repeated several times.

Throughout the operation, the wings and much of the net itself remain overboard.

Setting the Gear (See Fig. 11)

To begin resetting the gear, the cod-end is placed in the water, the bullrope is retied to the headline, and the quarter ropes fastened once more at the

Fig. 11. Side trawling setting operation.

Top left: cod end and mouth have been put overboard and quarters unhooked. The bullrope has been tied to the headline and here the quarter rope is being paid out.

Middle: the quarter rope has been tied to the wing end and the net allowed to float away from the vessel.

Right: the winch brakes are released and the ground cable runs out through the Kelly's eye. Here the stopper is about to seat in the eye.

Bottom left: doors are unhooked, the vessel put ahead and the net streams out. Floats and wing can be seen at surface.

Middle: the doors have been eased out a few feet and are "flying" just before winch brakes are released to set the gear.

Right: when required length of warp is out, forward and after warps are pulled together to rail by means of grapnel and messenger.

Fig. 11 (cont'd).
Left: messenger is led through snatch block to starboard warping drum and warps heaved up to the rail.
Right: once the warps have been heaved in, they are placed together in the towing clamp. When any slight adjustments to
ensure equal warp length have been made, towing commences.

wings. Twine and the mouth of the net taken aboard are put out, the quarters of the net released, and the quarter ropes allowed to run out. While this is done the vessel is maintained beam-on to the wind with very little or no way-on to ensure she drifts away from the gear, minimizing the likelihood of fouling the propeller. The vessel now moves slowly ahead, turning to the side at which the net is being worked so that a strain is placed on the ground cables. The brakes on the winch drums are released, allowing the ground cables to run out through the Kelly's eye until they are held by the stopper jamming in the eye. The towing pull is now taken by the doors which are still hooked to the gallows, and the warps are clipped to the otter board towing brackets.

The winch drums now heave in the warps slightly to take the pull of the doors off the dog chains, which may then be unhooked from the doors. At this point, the pull of the trawl gear is transferred entirely to the warps which are then run out a few feet from the winch drums so the otter boards are "flying" just above the water surface and all is ready to set the doors.

Speed is now increased, the vessel put into a more acute turn so that the net swings out. At a given signal the winch drum brakes are released, the drag of the gear pulling out the warps so that the doors enter the water and open the net's mouth. Once the warps are running out smoothly, the vessel is straightened up and the warps run out evenly from the drums. When marks on the warps indicate the

required length is out, the winch brakes are applied and it remains to place the warps in the towing block.

To accomplish this, a grapnel is attached to a messenger line taken through conveniently located blocks to the starboard warping drum. This grapnel is thrown so that both warps are caught and they are then pulled up to the towing block and clamped in place. Once this is done any slight adjustments needed to ensure equal lengths of warp lead to both doors may be made, and the tow is commenced.

First and Last Tows

The procedures described are those for hauling and setting the gear while actually fishing, and the operations of getting the gear overboard when commencing and retrieving it on terminating fishing need consideration.

While the vessel is steaming to the grounds or changing grounds the doors are stowed between the gallows and the bulwarks, the net being laid along the deck inside the bulwarks. To begin fishing the doors must be put overboard and hung on the dog chains. This may be achieved by means of a strop which is attached to the door bracket, run up and over the top gallows sheave and heaved by a whip from overhead. This pulls the door up, and it may then be pushed outboard and hooked up. The doors are brought inboard in a similar fashion (see Fig. 12). The net is usually put overboard by hand with the aid of a whip from overhead if needed.

When bringing the net aboard, the procedure is similar to that described previously, up to the time when the mouth is brought aboard. After this has been done, the body is pulled in as far as possible by hand, and then a strop is placed round the net as far down as possible over the side, heaved up by

Fig. 12. Preparation and recovery of gear aboard side trawler.
Top: getting in the after door.
Bottom: fleeting the net.

the overhead whip and dumped inboard (see Fig. 12). This procedure, known as "fleeting" is continued until the main part of the net is aboard and each wing is then treated similarly. The net is laid inside the bulwark.

Equipment Required for Side Trawling

1. Winch

At least two main drums and two warping heads (Fig. 13). The drums must have the required warp capacity and sufficient pulling power.

An element of danger is present in the use of warping heads or "gypsies" expecially when large loads are worked, so that many modern winches are built with four drums, two of which are used for the warps and two for handling the pulls normally taken on the warping heads. Warping heads are usually fitted in order that several pulls may be taken at the same time.

2. Warp and Door Handling

(a) Deck bollards (Fig. 13) arranged to provide a good run of warps from the winch to the gallows. A distance of at least 12 feet from the winch to the nearest bollard is desirable to permit easy spooling of the warps on the drum.

(b) Gallows frames (Fig. 13) well stayed and with a sheave at the base, and a top or towing block arranged to provide a convenient run of the warps. A dog chain with a hook at the free end should be attached to the gallows for hooking up the doors.

3. Quarter Rope Handling

(a) Open sheaves or snatchblocks arranged between the gallows and above the rails to take the quarter ropes (Fig. 13); typically these may be some 24 feet apart longitudinally and some 3 feet above the rail. These blocks may be hung from frameworks associated with the gallows, or on posts on the rail.

(b) Arrangement of snatchblocks to lead the quarter ropes to the warping heads.

4. Net and Cod-End Handling

(a) At least one single whip hung either from the mast or from overhead gear. Usually two are available (Fig. 13).

(b) At least one three-part falls hung from the mast or overhead gear. Again, two are usually available (Fig. 13).

5. Towing Block and Associated Gear

(a) Towing block (see Fig. 13) hung on a length of chain securely fastened inboard of the bulwark aft.

(b) Snatchblock arranged to provide a lead for the messenger to the starboard warping head. Normally the snatchblocks are arranged so that they may be used for several purposes and often a maximum of three, suitably positioned, will allow for the necessary runs of quarter ropes, bullrope, and messenger.

It is possible to devise various alternative deck layouts that will provide a reasonably efficient side trawling operation. The layout chosen for a particular vessel will depend on whether trawling only is to be carried out, or whether the capability of using other fishing methods is desired. Two common arrangements are shown in Figures 14, 15 and 16 for vessels in the United Kingdom.

The booms are used for other fishing methods, and the use of boom-mounted sheaves for quarter rope handling during trawling obviates the permanent mounts, which would need removing when not trawling.

Crew

On vessels up to about 80 feet in length, the gear may be worked by three crew members—one on the winch, one at the forward gallows who also attends to the towing block, and one in the wheelhouse who also attends the after gallows. This presupposes that the catch can be cleaned and stowed by this number between hauls. If the catch requires considerable attention, then this may dictate a larger crew, as also may trips of more than a week's duration. Often, a vessel will carry four crew, with three on deck at one time while the fourth man is resting.

STERN TRAWLING

Whereas the side trawler sets and hauls the trawl gear over the side, and tows from gallows and a towing block on that side, the stern trawler carries out all these operations over the stern.

Several distinctive means of handling gear have emerged as stern trawling has gained in popularity and as techniques and gear have developed.

Typical Layout

Although the method of gear handling may differ, the general layout of most vessels is similar. Small stern trawlers are usually single decked with transom stern, although at the upper end of the size scale a shelter deck or very long forecastle may be utilized. They are characterized by a wide, clear, working deck aft with wheelhouse and living accommodation forward sited above and/or abaft the forecastle. (See Figs. 17, 21, etc.)

The engine room is usually forward beneath the deckhouse with sleeping accommodation forward of it, and the fish rooms lie below the working deck. Abaft the fish rooms, fuel and water tanks are often fitted to allow control of trim as the loading varies during a voyage. Some vessels have the engine room aft and the fish holds further forward, the uptakes being brought up at the side of the working deck.

The winch is sited abaft the deckhouse, which will often include space for the skipper, and a messroom as well as the wheelhouse. The gear is towed from gallows sited aft on each side of the stern.

Stern trawlers offer two striking advantages when compared with side trawlers:

(a) As the gear is worked over the stern, the vessel is maintained on a straight course while hauling and setting, the pull being along the direction of motion. In most cases the vessel can therefore be headed directly into the wind and sea, and will be able to continue fishing under more severe conditions than a side trawler, so permitting a greater proportion of the voyage time to be utilized for fishing.

(b) The working area at the after end of the vessel is much steadier, being less affected by pitching, and the forward deckhouse provides protection and hence greater safety and comfort for the crew.

The main methods of gear handling found aboard a stern trawler are:

1. Use of quarter ropes in a similar manner to the side trawler, but worked over the stern.
2. Net drum.
3. Stern ramp.
4. Various combinations of the above.

Stern Trawling Using Quarter Ropes

This method utilizes essentially the same arrangement of trawl and handling gear as in side trawling, and is illustrated in Figure 17. The procedure is similar to that for side trawling except that it is carried out over the stern.

When towing, the warps are taken from the main winch drums over towing blocks hung from gallows (often of the cantilever type) each side of the transom stern.

Fig. 13. Side trawling . . . deck gear.

Top left: the working deck looking forward.

Middle: looking aft. The warps run forward from the winch and around deck bollards. The port warp runs through sheave at base of gallows and over gallows block. The warps run forward further deck bollard inside bulwark to after gallows. When aboard, the net is stowed in the checker running inside bulwark.
Starb'd warp is taken round further deck bollard inside bulwark to after gallows.

Right: winch with two main drums for warps and two warping heads. More modern winches have self-spooling devices to wind warp evenly on drum.

Bottom left: more detailed view shows starb'd drum and warping drum. Starb'd warp runs over sheave at gallows base to gallows block. Deck snatch-block is seen in foreground.

Middle: gallows sheave.

Right: quarter rope sheaves. Forward sheave hangs from boom. After sheave from post on rail. The snaphook for hooking up after quarter is seen on post.

Fig. 13 (cont'd).
Left: whip and falls are suspended on wires between mast and after structure. The sail is for steadying purposes.
Right: towing clamp; the clamp is hinged at left and held closed by pin when warps are in place.

Hauling Back

When hauling back, the winch heaves the doors up to the gallows where they are disconnected and left hanging; heaving is now continued, the stopper pulled out of the Kelly's eye and the sweeplines run through the eye until the wings reach the gallows (Fig. 17). The quarter ropes are now detached from the wings and attached to messengers run over blocks on the gantry. The pull is taken either by auxiliary drums or the warping heads of the winch, and the mouth of the net pulled inboard.

While the main body of the net remains in the water over the stern, lines from the straps at x and y are now untied from the headline and taken to the winch in order to lift the catch aboard. If the catch is light, it may be brought aboard in the cod-end in one pull, if splitting is required, then a pull is first taken at x to force the fish into the cod-end which is then brought aboard. When empty, the cod-end is refastened and put back into the water to be refilled by another pull on x. These operations are continued until all the catch is aboard.

During the hauling operation, the vessel steams slowly ahead, usually into the wind and sea so that the pull is straight over the stern. When the catch is being brought aboard, speed is reduced further to aid recovery, but the direction is maintained, so providing a safer, steadier and drier working platform for the operation.

Setting the Gear

When the gear is to be set, the vessel steams along the desired course, into wind and sea if desirable. The cod-end is thrown out and the working ropes retied in their correct positions on headline and wings, the mouth is lifted out with assistance from overhead as necessary, and the net streamed out astern; the sweeplines run out through the Kelly's eye until the stopper seats. Once the doors are connected to the warps and unhooked from the gallows, all is ready for setting. This may be accomplished by releasing the winch brakes simultaneously, so allowing the doors to drop into the water and spread while "on the run", or alternatively the warps may first be eased out until the doors are just below the surface and seen to be spreading satisfactorily before the warps are released and allowed to run out to the required extent. In either case the vessel is often slowed before the winch is braked in order to reduce the sudden shock as the warps take the net drag. The winch is now braked securely, and towing commenced.

First and Last Tows

The procedure for getting the gear overboard and aboard is similar to that described for side trawling.

Equipment Required

This method is common in Europe, and the vessels are characterized by the trawl winch mounted abaft the deckhouse or forecastle, and the heavy gantry aft for handling the gear.

Winch—Should have at least two main drums and two warping heads. Modern practice tends to a four-drum winch having two main and two auxiliary drums which are used for the quarter ropes and bag handling ropes; this provides for a safer operation than using warping heads; it is usual, however, to fit warping heads for any general duties.

In order to ensure a working deck clear of running wires, the winch may be mounted at forecastle level so that the wires run over the heads of crew members on the working deck.

Towing and Handling Warps and Doors

A good run of warps from the winch to the gallows is necessary, and the required blocks and sheaves must be arranged to permit easy spooling on the winch and a satisfactory run over the gallows blocks with a minimum of direction changes.

A pair of gallows may be mounted at each side of the working deck aft, often of cantilever type; alternatively, the towing supports may be incorporated into the gantry structure which will leave the bulwarks completely free, but may allow the doors to move dangerously in a seaway.

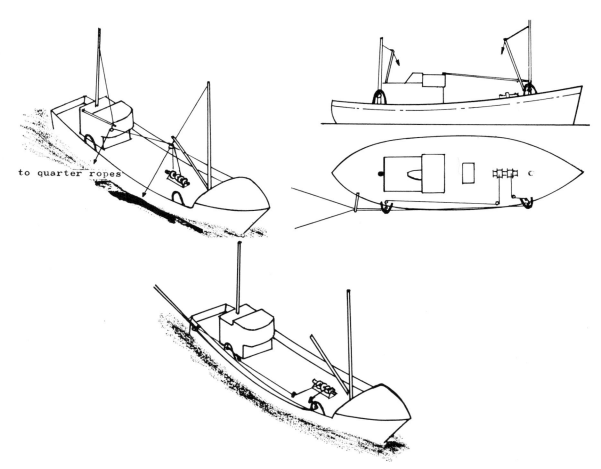

to quarter ropes

Fig. 14. Alternative layout for small side trawler. Another common arrangement where the winch is mounted fore and aft, booms being used to work quarter ropes.
Top left: quarter rope handling.
Top right: towing.
Bottom: deck plan of warp layout while towing.

Crew

Normally, at least four men are required to work the gear, but in small vessels or in ships where the winch controls are in the wheelhouse, a crew of three is sufficient. Additional crew will be required if more than minimum attention is required to the catch before stowing.

Advantages

Very little handling of the net is involved when fishing, but if repairs are necessary, a fleeting operation must be undertaken in order to bring it aboard. As the main part of the net is left in the water, there is a possibility of fouling the propeller or rudder.

Very little deck space is needed beyond that for dumping, sorting, and cleaning the catch, this makes the method suitable for small vessels.

Size of Vessels

This method is used on vessels as small as 35 feet overall and up to 125 feet or more in length, the equipment may vary to suit the needs and size of particular vessels.

Fig. 15. Scottish side trawler with fore and aft mounted winch.

As the gallows blocks are the effective towing points for the warps, they must be mounted sufficiently forward of the rudder axis to allow the vessel adequate manoeuvrability, but not so far forward that the warps can foul the stern when turning sharply.

An unstayed gantry or fishing mast, single or biped, may be positioned at the after part of the working deck; the blocks for working gear are usually mounted on a cross member to provide direct leads to the auxiliary winch drums; the net handling may be assisted if these blocks are situated on an outrigger extending aft from the cross member. Depending on the size of the vessel, positioning of the mast, and the size of the net, a roller mounted on the cross member may be necessary in order to take a sufficiently long pull on the webbing. Alternatively, a pivoted gantry may be utilized; this is discussed further in the stern ramp section.

Stern Trawling With Net Drum

Vessel and Gear

This method originated on the west coast of Canada and the United States, and is an extremely effective means of handling reasonably large and heavy gear on a small vessel. The layout of these vessels may be seen from Figures 19, 21, 23.

The winch is mounted abaft the deckhouse so that the warps run out athwartships and around heavy sheaves mounted on the rails; from those sheaves they are taken over towing blocks mounted on gallows (normally of cantilever type) at the stern and so to the doors.

At the stern, some two feet clear of the transom bulwark, is mounted a powered net reel on which the net is rolled when on board. A heavy boom, carrying whip and falls, is hung from a mast at the after end of the deckhouse and used for bringing the catch aboard.

Connections between the warps, doors, independent cables and ground cables differ from those for the trawling methods described previously. In this method the warps are shackled permanently to the doors and the inboard end of the independent cable is connected to the warps, just above their connection to the doors, by a G-clip and flat link arrangement. No Kelly's eye is used, the ends of the ground cables being attached to the door brackets by G-clips; the outboard end of the independent cable is shackled permanently to the ground cable (see Fig. 18).

Operation

The method of operation is illustrated in Figures 19 and 20.

Hauling

When hauling, the otter boards are hove up to the gallows and left hanging on the warps, being clamped if necessary to prevent slamming. The independent cables are now unhooked from the warps and clipped to eyes on the drum which then winds them up until the pull of the trawl is taken; at this point the backstrap is disconnected from the ground cables and hung on the gallows.

Ground cables, wings, and belly of the trawl are now wound on to the drum, leaving the length required to get the cod-end aboard for emptying. The cod-end is now taken round to the ship's side, and brought aboard, utilizing whip and falls from the overhead boom (see Fig. 19).

For most of the hauling sequence the vessel is steaming ahead, into wind and sea if necessary, and

Fig. 16. British side trawler bringing the net aboard. Note the V-type doors.

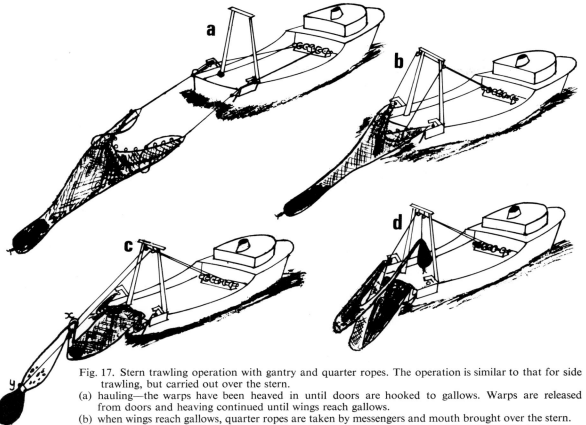

Fig. 17. Stern trawling operation with gantry and quarter ropes. The operation is similar to that for side trawling, but carried out over the stern.

(a) hauling—the warps have been heaved in until doors are hooked to gallows. Warps are released from doors and heaving continued until wings reach gallows.

(b) when wings reach gallows, quarter ropes are taken by messengers and mouth brought over the stern.

(c) when mouth is aboard, the bullrope and strap are taken by messenger and the net brought to the stern.

(d) the bag is brought back aboard by bullrope and whip and splitting carried out over the stern.

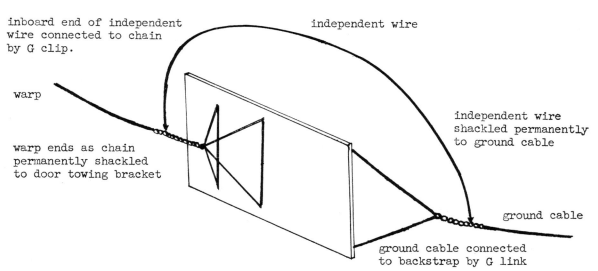

Fig. 18. Towing and independent wire arrangement for drum and ramp trawling.

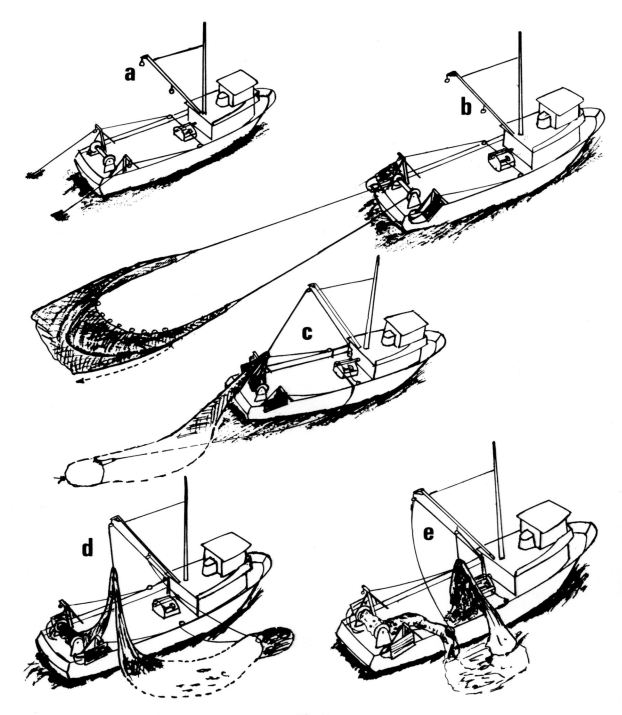

Fig. 19

the pull is taken fore and aft along the direction of travel. The craft is manoeuvred, however, in order to bring the cod-end alongside and aboard. The splitting operation is carried out over the side using whip and falls.

Setting

When setting the gear, the vessel is maintained on a straight course; first, the cod-end is put over the stern and the drum turned to wind off the body of the net, which is pulled out by the drag. The mouth and bottom gear is put overboard, with the aid of a whip from the boom if necessary, and the drum continues to revolve until the ground cables are out; it is then stopped to allow them to be clipped to the backstraps. Winding out is continued slowly until the doors take the pull, then stopped to allow the inboard end of the independent cables to be disconnected from the drum and clipped to the warps. All is now ready to set the doors and run out the warps to their required extent.

Crew

On a small vessel, two men can manage the gear, as it is possible for the helmsman to duplicate his duties, especially if the winch and drum controls are in the wheelhouse. Only one man is needed astern at the drum and he can handle the cod-end while the other works the winches and manoeuvres the vessel. On larger ships, or if the winch controls are not in a wheelhouse having a clear view of the working deck, it is desirable to have one man on the wheel, with one on the winch in addition to at least one on the working deck, remembering the heavier gear involved.

Advantages

Although the cod-end is brought over the side and therefore the vessel must be turned beam on to the sea at times, this method enables a vessel to handle a heavier gear than might be normal for its size, and makes a "big" trawler out of a boat too small to utilize the trawl-ramp method effectively. There is no manhandling of the web, and although the cod-end must be lifted aboard it is reasonably simple to split large tows. As the bulk of the trawl is stowed on the drum, the working deck is kept clear even on relatively small vessels and the net can easily be wound off the drum for repairs, if necessary.

Due to the athwartship leads from the winch, there are no running lines or wires crossing the deck and the drum assists in making the operation trouble free and safe.

Size of Vessel

As the net is wound aboard on to the drum, deck space required is limited to that for the drum mounting plus the area needed to dump, clean, and sort the catch. The method is therefore very suitable for vessels of 40 feet overall, or less, while designs have reached 90 feet.

Equipment

Winch—Requires at least two main drums for the warps, and two warping heads for handling the cod-end. In place of utilizing the warping heads for the cod-end handling, the warps may be linked inboard of the rail sheave; the doors may now be hung on the gallows, the warps disconnected at the links and used as messengers for the cod-end handling. Due to the short distances between rail sheaves and the winch drums, self-spooling arrangements are desirable.

Trawl Drum—Must be large enough to wind on the trawl and bottom gear if fitted. Figure 21 shows a drum with a single flange at each end, and in this case the ground cables are wound on to the centre drum and the net on top of them. A further development can be seen in Figure 20 where a second

---

Fig. 19. Operation of stern drum trawler.
(a) when towing, the warps pass athwartships from the winch, round rail mounted sheaves to the gallows and so to the doors.
(b) when hauling, the doors are pulled up to the gallows and remain attached to the warps. Independent wires are disconnected from towing bracket and connected to leads from drum. Drum rotates to take pull, ground cables are disconnected from backstrap and wound on to drum.
(c) the mouth and part of body are wound on drum. Ring strap is used to lift body by overhead falls. Vessel begins turn to starboard, bullrope being taken forward to bring cod end alongside.
(d) with trawl alongside, the body is lifted to fill cod end. Cod end lift is taken by second whip or falls (splitting operation).
(e) full cod end is lifted and dumped. It is then returned to the water and filled again by lifting the body. Operation is repeated until all catch is aboard.

Fig. 20. Hauling sequence aboard a small stern drum trawler.

Top left: the doors are heaved up to the gallows and remain attached to the warps. They may be secured to prevent banging. The independent wire has been unhooked from the G clip seen loose here, and clipped to the drum. The drum winds in until it takes the pull of the net and the backstraps are hanging loose.

Middle: the backstraps are unhooked from the ground cable.

Right: the drum reels in the ground cable and bridle until just before the wing comes aboard, they are passed through from the flanges to the main drum and reeling is continued.

Bottom left: the drum reels in place on the drum. Here the mouth is in place on the drum.

Middle left: the net lying astern during reeling. The bottom gear is about to come aboard.

Middle right: the bottom gear and body are reeled in until the cod end can be brought alongside.

Right: the cod end is brought aboard by tackle from the boom above.

Fig. 21. 75-ft. stern drum trawler. This vessel has a drum without flanges and is using V-type doors.

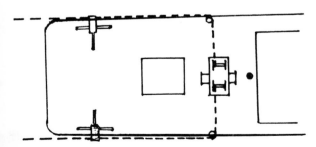

Fig. 22. Transverse winch mounting for stern trawling. This arrangement leaves the deck free of working wires, an important factor in small vessels.

flange has been added at each end of the drum so that the ground cables are wound on to the drum between the flanges; slots cut through the inner

flanges allow the wires to be passed through on to the main drum when the wings start to come aboard.

Rail Sheaves—Either open or closed with a gate to allow the warps to be removed. These are sited on the rails opposite the winch drums; as the towing pull is taken at the sheaves, they must be mounted on a firm supporting structure. Good practice requires their effective diameter to be at least 16 times the warp diameter.

Gallows—Sited each side of the after deck, they are usually of the tripod cantilever type and often are made portable, being pinned into sockets at their base.

Boom—The boom must be of sufficient length to bring the cod-end aboard in the required position, and is usually stayed on the centre line. A separate topping winch for the boom may be found useful.

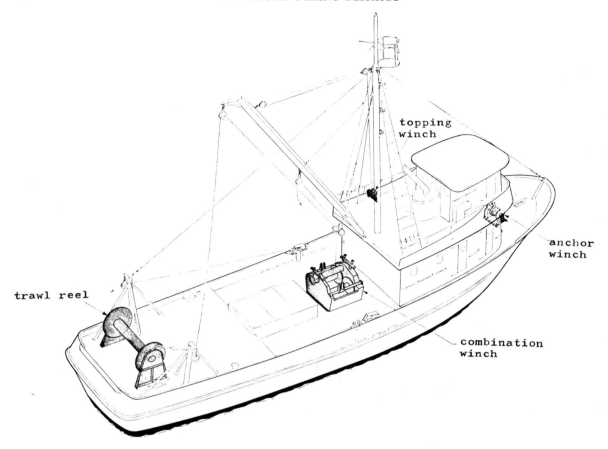

Fig. 23. Layout of small stern drum trawler.

Stern Ramp Trawling

Vessel and Gear

The principal feature of these vessels is the ramp at the stern leading from the waterline to deck level up which the cod-end and catch is pulled. Possibly the most important advantage of the arrangement is that the cod-end does not have to be lifted over the stern or side, but need merely be elevated for emptying, making for a relatively simple splitting operation.

The methods used in handling the gear and trawl vary considerably, but in nearly all cases the complete net is hauled aboard. Basically, three procedures arise, various combinations of equipment being possible for each.

(a) Wings of Trawl Taken up Each Side of the Working Deck

This, perhaps the most common arrangement, is illustrated in Figures 25–27 which show various combinations of deck layout and equipment. The trawl net, doors and warp arrangement is similar to that for stern drum trawling.

The basis of the method is the provision of bobbin trays port and starboard of the working deck, each of sufficient length to accommodate half the head rope. The inboard coamings of these curve and meet at their after end to suit the shape of the mouth and to contain the heavy bottom gear in a seaway.

Figure 25 shows one arrangement utilizing an

Fig. 24. Operations aboard a stern drum trawler.
Top: setting the trawl. Floats show the headline, and the rubber discs of the groundrope can be seen.
Bottom: splitting operation aboard a 76-ft. vessel.

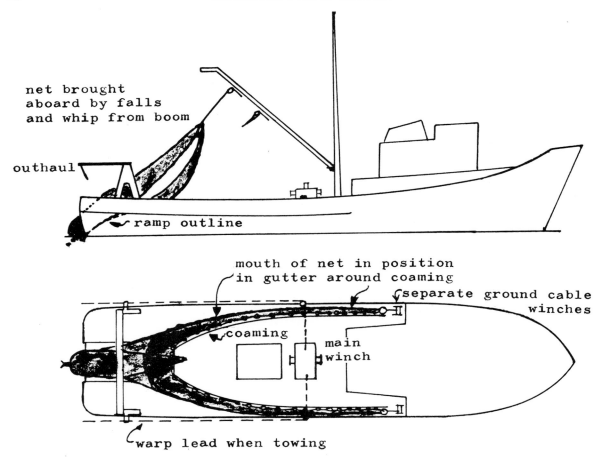

net brought
aboard by falls
and whip from boom

outhaul

ramp outline

mouth of net in position
in gutter around coaming

separate ground cable
winches

coaming

main
winch

warp lead when towing

Fig. 25. Stern ramp trawler. 80 to 90 ft. overall, with wings of net brought up each side of the working deck. Here, a winch with athwartships leads is used, and the cod end is hauled by a third drum taken over the boom blocks.

athwartship mounted main winch to handle the warps in the same manner as in drum trawling. Here, small single drum winches are fitted at the forward end of each bobbin tray to handle the ground cables.

Hauling

The hauling sequence begins with the doors being hove up to the gallows by the main winch; the independent cables are then disconnected from the warps, passed over to lie in the ramp opening, and connected to leads from the single drum winches; these winches now take the pull and, once the door backstraps have been disconnected from the ground cables, pull the mouth of the net up the ramp and hence to the position shown in Figure 25. When the headrope is hard against the tray coaming, the cod-end is hauled up the ramp by means of the bullrope and straps as necessary, and lifted over the belly lying in the ramp for emptying forward of the after end of the coaming.

Often a third drum will be provided on the winch for cod-end handling, and is used in conjunction with overhead blocks on the boom.

Usually a gate will be fitted at the top of the ramp. As a safety measure against seas coming up the ramp and flooding the working deck, this gate is normally closed, but drops flush with the deck while gear is being worked. The whole length of the net must therefore be pulled aboard forward of the gate to allow its closure; this is achieved by means of straps at convenient points in the webbing

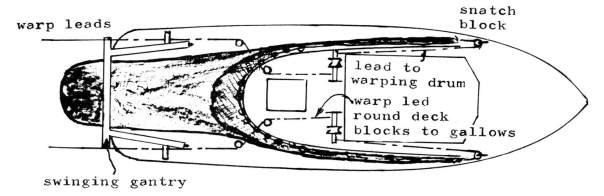

Fig. 26. Arrangement using pivoted gantry.

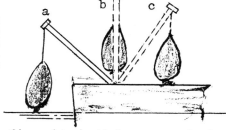

Top: small stern ramp trawler utilizing traditionally mounted winch where the ground cables are hauled onto auxiliary drums through snatch blocks forward. This sketch also shows the pivoted (swinging) gantry used to handle the webbing and cod end. Winch is mounted with aft warp leads led by deck bollards to towing blocks.

Middle: use of pivoted or swinging gantry:
   (a) cod end hooked up to gantry;
   (b) gantry swinging forward;
   (c) in position for emptying.

Bottom: The pivoted gantry is shown in the forward stowed position. In this vessel, towing blocks are mounted outboard of gantry uprights instead of separate gallows. In this case no stern ramp is fitted, the net being brought aboard by quarter ropes.

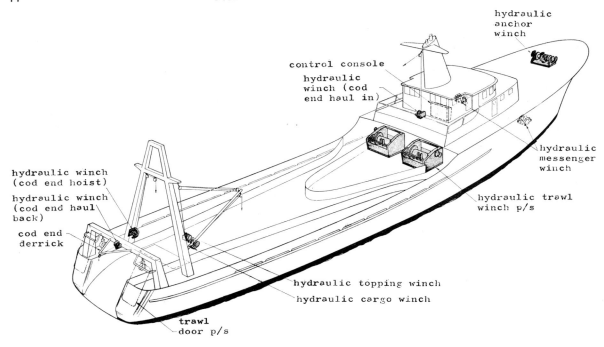

hydraulic
anchor
winch

control console

hydraulic
winch (cod
end haul in)

hydraulic winch
(cod end hoist)

hydraulic winch
(cod end haul
back)

cod end
derrick

hydraulic
messenger
winch

hydraulic trawl
winch p/s

hydraulic topping winch

hydraulic cargo winch

trawl
door p/s

Fig. 27. Arrangement of larger stern ramp trawlers. Approximately 115 ft. and above.
Top: this arrangement utilizes separate warps and ground cable winches. The vessel is too large for boom hoisting to be
   employed, so that a stern gantry is fitted. The cod-end derrick is used to haul out the net while setting and the cod end
   is hauled up the ramp by the cod end haul-in winch and lead forward.
Bottom: 132 ft. stern ramp trawler. In this case a standard type of four drum trawl winch has been placed at forecastle
   deck level so that warps and working wires run clear of the working deck while providing good leads to the towing
   blocks on the transverse stern gantry.

to which are attached lines, enabling the net to be drawn up by tackles from the overhead boom before the cod-end is lifted.

An alternative arrangement is shown in Figure 26. Here, a traditional winch, mounted to provide a fore and aft pull, is fitted. The main drums pull the doors up to the gallows; the independent cable is then disconnected from the warps and taken by a lead through snatch blocks forward and so to auxiliary drums on the winch; once the backstraps are disconnected from the ground cables, the wings can be brought aboard until the mouth of the net seats round the coaming.

Figure 26 also shows the use of a swinging or pivoted gantry to bring the cod-end aboard; the gantry is shown in its fully aft position; the webbing and cod-end are handled by blocks on the cross member of the gantry, which is then swung forward so that the cod-end is aboard, and may be emptied using an overhead block.

Figure 27 shows arrangements aboard larger stern ramp trawlers where the length of the working deck is too great to allow use of a boom. Fixed gantries support blocks used for cod-end handling. Both split winch and standard winch arrangements are illustrated. The cod-end is first pulled up the ramp by a line from a high fixed point forward and then handled by blocks on the gantry.

Setting

Usually, a cod-end haul-out arrangement is necessary to pull the cod-end back down the ramp and into the water, so that it can assist in dragging out the body and mouth when the winches are released. For this purpose a line is taken over a block mounted at the extreme after end of the vessel, often on an outrigger from the stern (see Fig. 27); one end of the line is hooked to the cod-end, the other being taken to a warping head. When setting, the ramp gate is lowered, the cod-end and some webbing hauled out and then the ground cables run out until the doors can be hooked up; the doors can now be set and the warps run out to their required length while the vessel steams on a straight course.

Advantages

The arrangement where the wings are taken up each side of the working deck ensures that the net is well spread out for repairs, and the bobbins being contained by the gutter and coaming cannot roll around in bad weather. Often, depending on the size of the vessel, the net can be brought aboard in

two pulls, and is always well clear of the fish pounds on deck so that the gear can be set immediately after emptying without interfering with men working on the catch. Although the cod-end must be dragged over the bottom gear and floats for emptying, this does not appear to cause undue wear, and the main winch can be placed under cover. The ramp gate is an important safety factor for a stern ramp vessel, especially in small craft with low freeboard, as it eliminates the likelihood of flooding the main deck by seas breaking up the ramp.

On large stern trawlers it is usual for a shelter deck to be fitted, and the wet fish taken on board are usually passed below into the tweendeck for storage and processing. Small vessels do not normally have sufficient depth to allow the provision of tweendecks for this purpose, so that all fish are dumped into pounds on the deck for cleaning and sorting, leaving the crew exposed to the weather during this operation. Considerable protection to the crew on the working deck can be provided by fitting portable sides above the bulwarks between the break of forecastle and the gallows, an important item in northern areas in the winter with attendant wind and spray.

Size of Vessel

Stern ramp trawling has become an established method on vessels above some 150 feet, but only during the last few years has it become accepted aboard small vessels.

Vessels of only 80 feet overall can handle trawls up to 110-foot groundrope length fitted with rough bottom gear; this lower limit of size will, of course, depend on the length required between the ground-cable winches and the after end of the gutter coaming, and is therefore controlled by the necessity to match the size of the net and the gutter length available. There is a limit as to how far forward the ground-cable winches can be placed, due to accommodation requirements, on most vessels.

(b) Both Wings Taken up One Side of the Working Deck

Figure 28 shows one arrangement for this type of vessel, in which a bobbin tray is fitted at one side of the working deck to hold both wings complete with headrope and groundrope with bottom gear. This tray or gutter must be of sufficient size to contain the bobbins and rollers, and of sufficient length to handle the doubled footrope, which is held round a post at its after end. A two-drum winch is fitted

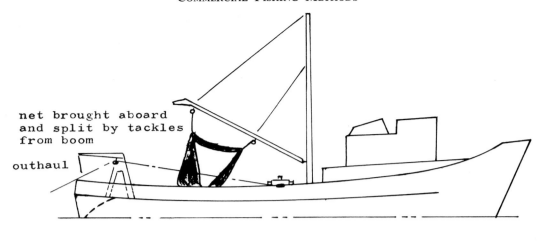

net brought aboard
and split by tackles
from boom

outhaul

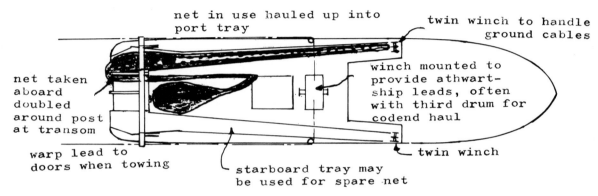

net in use hauled up into
port tray

twin winch to handle
ground cables

winch mounted to
provide athwart-
ship leads, often
with third drum for
codend haul

net taken
aboard
doubled
around post
at transom

warp lead to
doors when towing

twin winch

starboard tray may
be used for spare net

Fig. 28. Stern ramp trawler where net is taken up tray on one side of working deck. A second net can be kept ready for
use in the other tray. This is particularly useful where nets of two designs may be used in a fishery.

at the forward end of the bobbin tray to handle the
ground cables, while a winch abaft the deckhouse
is used for the towing warps. Only the cod-end and
a portion of the webbing are brought up the ramp,
the net being doubled round a faired post at the
side of the ramp.

The operation is similar to the one where the
wings are brought up both sides of the deck, except
that one independent cable must be passed over to
the opposite side before being clipped to a lead from
the ground-cable winch.

The arrangement allows a second bobbin tray
to be placed on the other side of the working deck
to hold a spare net, so saving lost time when repairs
are necessary. For a trawl of 120-foot groundrope
length, the minimum practical length of vessel
would appear to be about 95 feet.

This system has been used for a number of vessels,

and appears to have originated in France, although
in a somewhat less sophisticated fashion, when the
deckhouse was placed to one side of the hull and
the net brought up the other side to give an "aircraft
carrier" look to the vessel.

Advantages

The method appears to have the advantages discussed in the previous section with several additions:
there is always a spare trawl ready for setting up
with no rigging required; once the spare trawl is
shot away, the other can be spread out for mending
without interfering with work on the catch. The
arrangement leaves the deck clear of the net mouth
and webbing so that the cod-end need not be
dragged over the net, floats and bottom gear.

The fishing operation requires only three men
including the winch operator, with a further man

necessary for icing if fish are stored round, or a further two if dressing is required before icing. A maximum crew of six would be required, including the Captain, for eight-day trips.

Equipment for Stern Ramp Trawling

Equipment required for the various alternative layouts has been detailed in the discussions; of particular interest, however, are:

Ramp—This may be a flat or curved surface extending from the waterline to the working deck. Width varies according to the size of the gear used from some 5·5 feet on smaller vessels to about 9·0 feet on ships of some 125 feet in length. Typical width for an 80-foot to 90-foot vessel might be in the order of 7·5 feet. The angle of the straight line joining the top and bottom points of the ramp varies between 30° and 35°; several designs are illustrated in Figure 29, and if curved, the profile may vary from a circular arc to one of varying radius of curvature, the radius being greatest at the bottom and gradually decreasing to deck level. The profile should be arranged so that the direction of pull for the cod-end when being brought up the ramp is at least tangential to the ramp at deck level; to prevent excessive damage to the catch and wear on the net, the pull should, if possible, be at a greater angle. Wherever possible the after end of the ramp should be in sight from the wheelhouse so that the skipper can view the complete operation.

Handling Cod-end—The pull of the cod-end must be at an angle as great as possible up the ramp, and this may be achieved on smaller vessels by use of a tackle from an overhead boom taken to the winch; this arrangement may also be used to elevate the cod-end to empty the catch.

In larger vessels, it is usual to mount a separate winch forward for the purpose of cod-end hauling up the ramp, and the lead is often taken over a block mounted at a height well above the winch, perhaps on a specially strengthened mast or funnel or at the top of the wheelhouse. For emptying, the cod-end will be elevated from a boom or overhead gantry having sufficient clearance from the deck to handle the length of cod-end on the largest net in use.

Stern Trawling Using Combination of Quarter-ropes, Ramp and Drum

(a) Combination of Ramp With Stern Drum

A number of vessels have been constructed, particularly on the east coast of the United States, in which an attempt has been made to combine a ramp and net drum, and so obtain the advantages of each.

A typical early arrangement is shown in Figure 30 where a drum is mounted coaxially with a winch arranged so that the warps lead aft. A ramp is fitted at the stern. In later designs, the net drum is located at various positions on the working deck between the ramp and winch; in some cases it is angled and set to one side of the vessel to provide greater deck space than possible in the early design.

When hauling, once the doors are at the gallows, the ground cable pull is transferred to the net drum in the usual fashion, and the net is then wound up

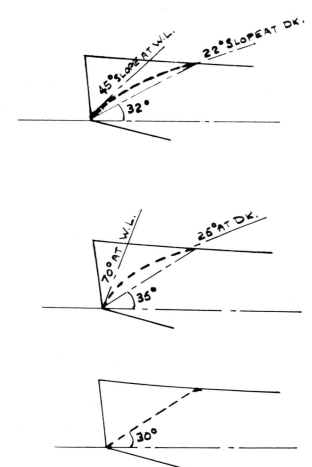

Fig. 29. Stern ramp profiles.
Top: circular arc.
Middle: varying radius.
Bottom: flat, faired at ends.

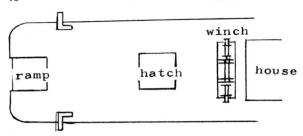

Fig. 30. Layout of stern trawler using ramp and drum. This is an early arrangement on the United States east coast vessels, where the net drum is integral with the main winch. Later designs placed the drum separately between the winch and ramp, or to one side of the deck, angled to lead correctly to the ramp.

on to the drum, heaving being continued until the cod-end is on the ramp or can be reached by a boom tackle for lifting and emptying.

As the net is pulled along the length of the working deck, some form of chute or gutter is required to prevent the bottom gear from rolling around, and fish must be dumped to one side of this. Hauling speed must be low to prevent excessive wear on the webbing as it is dragged along the deck, and practically all the net has to be on the drum before the cod-end can be reached for lifting.

A haul-back tackle is necessary to haul the gear aft for setting, and this will often necessitate successive fleeting operations; this may be lessened if the drum is mounted high above the deck.

The restricted deck space, due to the area taken up by the net and its chute, leaves little room for laying out the twine for repair, or for dumping fish into deck pounds.

The arrangement does have several advantages: the whole net is brought aboard in one pull and hence a minimum of handling is necessary, while the vessel steams a straight course; no special

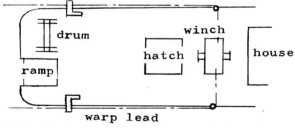

Fig. 31. Side-by-side mounting of ramp and drum aboard stern trawler. A more effective combination of net drum and ramp without loss of useful deck space and other problems inherent in the arrangement of Fig. 30. The net is reeled onto the drum and only the cod end hauled up the ramp.

winches are needed for handling the ground cables, while the cod-end can be lifted for emptying with a minimum of handling.

These advantages make the system apparently attractive to smaller vessels than would normally be able to use the ramp method, as only a 25 to 30 foot length of working deck would appear to be necessary.

The disadvantages of this particular arrangement appear to outweigh the advantages; discussions with skippers indicate that most of them are unhappy with the scheme, and in many cases have changed to some alternative way of handling the gear.

The principal advantages of the drum are its ability to store the net clear of the working area while allowing easy spreading for repair, and the very simple arrangement for hauling and setting without the necessity for a haulback.

An arrangement such as that of Figure 31 would eliminate most of the disadvantages of Figure 30 while gaining the advantages of both drum and ramp.

When hauling, the net would be wound on to the drum as in drum-trawling practice, but the cod-end is hauled up the ramp by a boom tackle or other arrangement, doubling the net round a post between drum and ramp. This does, however, require sufficient breadth of the deck at the stern to accommodate both net drum and ramp, while at the same time making for an unsymmetrical hauling arrangement.

A further variation requiring less deck width and allowing the haul to be along the centreline at all times is shown in Figure 32. In this system, the drum is mounted aft directly over the stern ramp. When hauling, the net is wound on to the drum in the usual way, but the cod-end is pulled up the ramp beneath the drum by a tackle from boom or mast. When setting, the cod-end is put back down the ramp, being drawn back into the water by the geometry of the layout, so that its drag can pull out the net as it is unwound from the drum.

This layout would appear to be ideal for vessels from 40 to 70 feet where other stern ramp methods cannot be used, and the present arrangements of winch and drum combinations have not proved satisfactory.

(b) Combination of Quarter Ropes and Ramp

The basis of this method is the use of the pivoted or fixed overhead gantry to lift only the cod-end up the ramp.

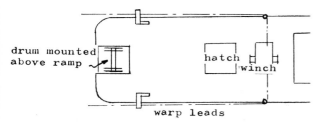

Fig. 32. Stern trawling arrangement with drum mounted above ramp. This provides a pull along the centreline at all times, and appears ideal, especially in vessels where insufficient transom width is available to utilize the side-by-side arrangement.

When hauling back, the quarter ropes are used to bring the net mouth aboard as described previously. The gantry or fishing mast is then utilized to drag the cod-end up the ramp rather than lift it bodily over the stern; this is the only difference between the procedure and that previously discussed.

A slightly greater distance between the transom and forward end of the working deck is required due to the space taken up by the ramp, but otherwise the method is subject to similar advantages and disadvantages as when the cod-end is lifted over the stern.

BOTTOM PAIR TRAWLING

Pair trawling (see Fig. 33), although perhaps in more common use during mid-water trawling, is also practised with the bottom trawl. Two boats, each towing one warp, are used; the net mouth is

kept open by the outward pull provided by correct lateral spacing of the vessels, so that no otter boards are required.

By utilizing the combined towing pull of the two vessels, and as no otter boards are needed, a larger net may be worked than would be possible by a single vessel; alternatively, two vessels of low horse-power, which could not undertake single boat otter trawling, can combine to use this method efficiently.

Net and Gear

As no doors are necessary, the trawl gear arrangements are simplified, the warps being connected directly to the bridles from each wing. Normally, a greater warp length/water depth ratio than for otter trawling is used; a ratio of 5:1 being common. The vessels maintain a distance apart that will provide the mouth opening and headline height found most effective for the gear and species being fished; an average lateral spacing is in the order of half the length of the warp run out.

The setting and hauling operations are carried out by one vessel, while the other is used only during the towing sequence; often each will take turns at these operations.

Hauling

When towing, the scene is that shown in Figure 33. When the time comes to haul back, both vessels haul on their warps until the bridles reach the gallows. The vessels then converge until they are a safe distance apart, and a heaving line is used to transfer a messenger line fastened to the bridle end on one vessel to the other; the first boat then disconnects the bridle from its warp so that the other may heave in the messenger on the winch through its second gallows block; when that bridle is hove up to the gallows, the net may be brought aboard and the cod-end emptied in the usual manner for the arrangement aboard. Either quarter ropes, a drum or ramp arrangement may be used.

Setting

When setting, the vessel with the net aboard sets it out with the bridles held at the gallows. The pull of one bridle is then transferred to the other boat by means of the heaving line and messenger, and the second vessel then connects its warp to that bridle.

Both vessels then steam ahead together, paying out the warps evenly to their required extent, and fishing commences.

Vessel

This method may be used by either side or stern trawlers outfitted for trawling; as there are no doors the operation is simplified, there being no need to transfer the pull from warps to ground cables via the independent cables.

Equipment required is, at the minimum, a single drum winch with two warping heads, the drum being used for the warp, and the warping heads for the messenger and to bring the cod-end aboard. It is usual, however, to fit out vessels when building so that they may undertake otter trawling in addition to pair trawling.

MULTI-RIG TRAWLING

In certain fisheries, multi-rig trawling, where several smaller trawls are towed in place of one large net, has been found particularly effective. The arrangement is of special importance in the shrimp and other fisheries, where the species are caught by scraping the bottom closely, and do not rise far from the sea bed. Two slightly differing operations may be found, typified by the "Gulf shrimp trawlers" of the United States, and European vessels which are often arranged to combine multi-rig with standard trawling methods.

Usually, two trawls are used, but several vessels have been built recently to tow three nets. The principal reason for using two nets rather than one large otter trawl is that in the type of fishing where species are caught on the bottom it is the width of the area scraped which determines largely the effectiveness of the rig, the height of the headrope above the seabed being less important.

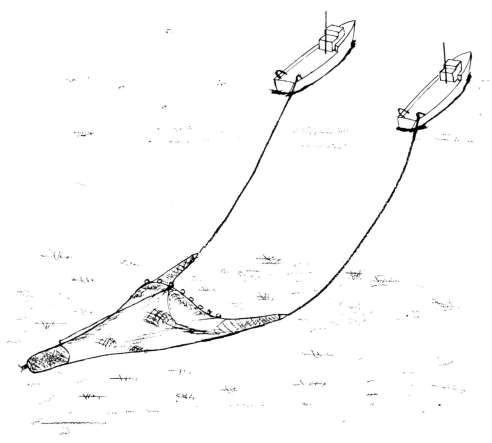

Fig. 33. Two boat bottom trawling. Each vessel handles one warp while towing. As the outward pull of the warps, due to lateral separation of boats, keeps the mouth open, otter boards are not necessary; the warps are connected directly to the bridles. The net is set out and retrieved by one vessel, the pull being transferred by a heaving line and messenger.

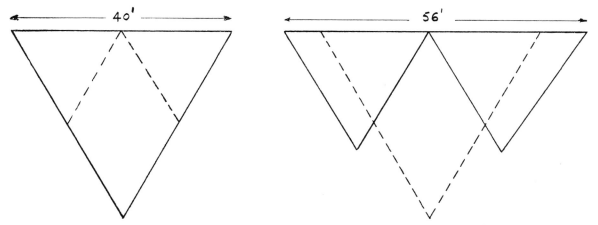

Fig. 34. Effectiveness of twin rig trawling. Illustrates in an exaggerated manner that:
Left: the same total net spread may be achieved with two trawls which, when combined, are appreciably smaller than the single trawl and consequently offer less towing resistance.
Right: the same power can be used to tow two nets giving a 30 to 40% greater horizontal spread than possible with a single net.

The same total net-spread can be achieved by two trawls which are together appreciably smaller than a single trawl and hence have less towing resistance; on the other hand, the same power needed for one large trawl can be used to tow two nets giving perhaps one-third greater horizontal spread; this is illustrated in an exaggerated and simplified manner in Figure 34.

Nets

Two distinct types of trawl gear are in common use—a small otter trawl and a beam trawl. In place of the two warps used for larger trawls, each net is towed by a single warp.

Twin-Rig Trawling Using Otter Trawls

This method is typified by the shrimp trawlers operating out of the Gulf of Mexico ports.

Trawl Gear

Figure 35 shows the arrangement of otter trawls used for twin-rig towing, the towing speed averaging about two knots.

Light trawl doors are connected directly to the wings by top and bottom wires, chain bridles being used in place of the steel bar towing brackets found on the heavier gear. A wire bridle runs from the warp end to each door towing-eye.

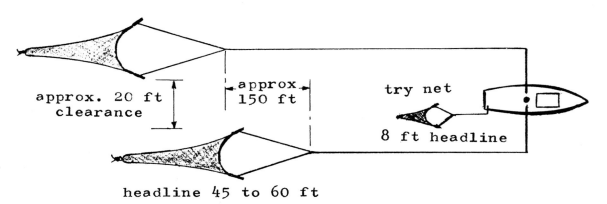

Fig. 35. Twin rig trawling. Gulf of Mexico double rig trawling using otter trawls. Each net is towed by a single warp and the starboard net is usually towed ahead. The "try" net is used to ensure the vessel "stays on shrimp".

The two nets are towed from the ends of outrigger booms on each side of the vessel, and it is usual to tow one net some 150 feet ahead of the other. Commonly, the trawls will have a headrope length of about 45 feet, although in more highly powered vessels a headrope length up to 80 feet may be utilized.

A feature peculiar to the Gulf shrimp fishery is the "try net", a small trawl equipped with miniature doors, which is used to sample the bottom for shrimp before the main trawls are put overboard. Being light and easily handled, the try net may be set, towed, and lifted by one man. Usually, it will be left overboard, being lifted at regular intervals while fishing to ensure that the vessel "stays on shrimp".

Fig. 36. Gulf of Mexico double rig shrimp trawler. Booms are often lowered while on passage.

Vessel Layout

Figures 36 to 41 show the deck layout of typical double-rig trawlers. The deckhouse, containing the wheelhouse and accommodation, is forward with the engine room beneath; a large working deck is provided aft by the use of a transom stern, and the winch or "hoister" is mounted at its forward end; the hold is situated below the working deck with a well-stayed mast amidships at the after end of the deckhouse. Twin booms are arranged, hinging outwards from the mast or house to provide outboard towing points for the nets. A heavy, permanently located and well-stayed "boom" is fitted abaft the mast with a crossmember at its tip, which supports several blocks for use in handling the nets. This boom is well supported and often a ratline arrangement will be fitted from the transom to this cross

member. In place of wire stays, the arrangement of Figure 40 is common where a firm steel structure is used to provide a form of inverted V when viewed from abeam.

The try net is towed from a separate davit aft, or from a block at mid-length of one of the outrigger booms, and handled by a drum on the main winch or by a separate winch.

Operation

The method of operation is shown in Figures 35, 37 and 38.

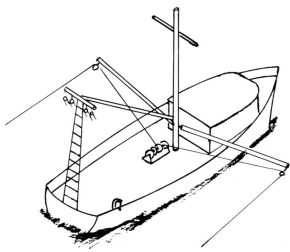

Fig. 37. Double rig vessel while towing. The warps are led from the winch to the towing blocks at boom ends and so to the door bridle. The small davit aft is used for handling the try net.

When towing (Figs. 35, 37) the outrigger booms are lowered by tackles from the masthead until the towing blocks at their tips are some 12 feet above the water surface in calm conditions; this prevents the ends of the outriggers from dipping into the water when the vessel rolls.

The warps are taken from the door bridle over towing blocks at the ends of the outriggers to the main winch drums.

Hauling

To commence hauling back, the winch man engages both drums simultaneously; the starboard trawl is usually towed ahead of the port trawl so that the former will be brought up to the towing block first; hauling is continued until the door towing bridle is brought in over the towing block and the doors are at the block.

Fig. 38. Double rig vessel hauling back. The doors are heaved up to the towing blocks and left hanging while the cod end only is brought aboard by overhead blocks.

A long boat hook is used to reach a lazy line attached to the cod-end strap, which is then hauled in by an overhead tackle on a warping drum; this tackle is used to lift the cod-end over the side and also to elevate it for dumping the catch (see Fig. 38).

The procedure is now repeated for the port trawl which by this time will be hauled up to the block. Throughout the hauling operation, the vessel is maintained on a straight course.

Setting

The setting operation is carried out while the vessel steams on a straight course; the cod-end is returned overboard, and when the winch brakes are released the net drag pulls the bridles and warps out through the towing blocks, and the port and starboard warps are run out to their correct extent.

First and Last Tows

On the first tow, the net is placed overboard by hand, the doors being lifted outboard with the aid of an overhead whip taken to a warping drum. At the end of fishing, a boathook is used to recover a tag line permanently secured to the doors in order to swing in the doors. The outriggers may now be hauled up to their stowed position by the topping lifts taken to a warping drum.

Equipment

Equipment required aboard a modern double-rig vessel using twin otter trawls and try net is illustrated in Figure 41.

Outriggers—These are mounted on the mast or deckhouse with goosenecks at their feet. They are guyed in a fore and aft direction by a tackle to the bulwark forward and to the boom cross member aft. A topping lift tackle is provided for raising and lowering the outrigger booms, which are usually constructed of steel piping stiffened as shown in the various illustrations.

When stowed, the outriggers are brought up to seat in supports at the ends of heavy cross trees on the mast. When running between fishing grounds they are often lowered to the fishing position to improve stability, and in heavy weather may be swivelled aft and lashed with their ends at deck level. The length of the outriggers is often about 24 feet when associated with a 45-foot headrope trawl.

Towing blocks—It is important that these are of sufficient width to allow the door towing bridles to pass through.

Winch—It has been common for the main winch to be of the three-drum type with two warping heads, mounted to provide transverse leads for the warps, two of the drums being used for the main net warps, the other for the try net, (see Fig. 39).

Fig. 39. Typical three drum winch used aboard shrimp trawlers in the Gulf of Mexico. The winch is driven through a power take-off from the main engine. The top drum is for handling the try net.

Fig. 40. More modern double rig shrimp trawler for Gulf of Mexico. Note the stiffening of the outrigger beams.

An alternative, having increasing application, is the use of a two-drum winch with two warping heads for the main net handling, with a separate try-net winch having its own warping head (see Fig. 41).

Net handling—Overhead tackles and whips should be mounted for use when putting net and doors overboard or for their recovery, and for handling the cod-end while bringing aboard and emptying.

The overhead blocks for these arrangements may be hung from the boom cross member or from a stay between the boom and mast.

Try net operation—The try net is towed either from a block supported on a small davit aft, or from a block at mid-length of one outrigger. In either case, convenient warp leads from the winch used must be arranged.

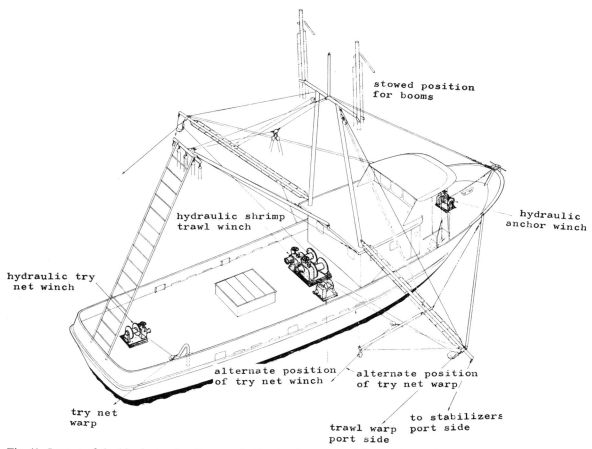

Fig. 41. Layout of double rig trawler. Two small otter trawls are towed from twin outrigger booms which are stowed vertically when steaming. Warps are handled by two drum winch abaft deckhouse and cod end is taken aboard by overhead whip and tackle taken to warping drums.

Twin-Rig Trawling Utilizing Beam Trawls

Typical of vessels utilziing this method are European trawlers operating out of Belgium and Holland.

Trawl Gear

The beam trawl is one of the earliest forms of trawl gear, being used extensively by sailing vessels before the steam age, and is a forerunner of the otter trawl as it is known today. Figure 42 shows the basic form of a beam trawl.

A heavy beam is supported by steel shoes at each end which run over the sea bed; the headrope is connected to the beam, the groundrope being fastened loosely between the bases of the shoes. The cod-end is formed in the usual manner, the strap having a lazy line attached to aid recovery.

The towing bridle is formed of three wires—one from each shoe and one from the centre of the beam. These come together and are shackled directly to the towing warp.

A number of advantages are claimed for the beam trawl in catching species which lie on the sea bed, including:

1. The length of warp has less influence on the beam trawl than with the otter trawl.

2. The opening does not change during course alterations.

3. The influence of tide is less than with the otter trawl.

4. Effectiveness of the gear is less affected by muddy bottoms than with the otter trawl.

A typical beam trawl may have a beam length of some 25 feet, with shoes to keep the beam some 2 feet off the sea bed.

Vessel Layout

The basic vessel layout for this method is similar to that described for the twin-rig vessel operating in the Gulf of Mexico fishery, except that, usually, the try net is absent (see Figs. 43–47).

Vessels using this method will often undertake stern trawling in addition and will have a low gantry fitted aft for towing this single trawl. When twin beam trawling, the gantry is utilized both to support the outrigger booms while steaming and to provide a mounting for blocks that are part of the warp lead arrangements.

The winch is usually of the four-drum type used in stern trawling, and is arranged to provide aft warp leads. Two drums are used for the warps and two for outrigger topping and net handling. A cargo

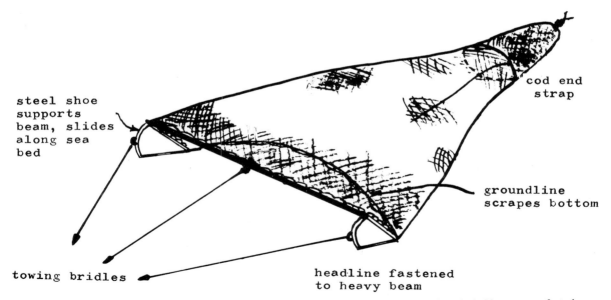

steel shoe supports beam, slides along sea bed

towing bridles

cod end strap

groundline scrapes bottom

headline fastened to heavy beam

Fig. 42. Beam Trawl. The headrope is fastened to a heavy boom, often about 25 ft. in length, held some two feet above the sea bed by steel shoes. The ground rope is connected loosely between the shoes so that it curves backwards. The cod end is formed in the usual manner with a strap so that it may be lifted for emptying. The towing warp is shackled to the treble bridle.

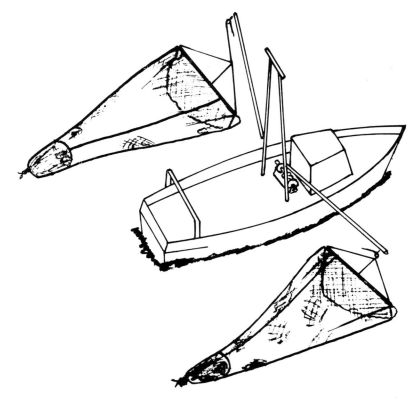

Fig. 43. Double rig trawling with beam nets. The winch is sited abaft the deckhouse and is of the four-drum type. This type of vessel is often used for stern trawling as well as double trawling. Only the cod ends are brought aboard for emptying by lazy lines attached to the cod end strap.

boom is arranged to provide supports for whip and falls used during net handling.

Operation

When towing, the outriggers or "fishing derricks" are set at the almost horizontal position and inclined slightly aft. If one net should hang up, the force at the boom tip is great enough at best to cause a problem with vessel handling, and at the worst may capsize the vessel. This may be counteracted by a particular arrangement of warp leads developed in Europe; the warps are led from the winch drum to a block mounted on the after gallows/gantry and so over the outrigger towing blocks to the net. The towing block is attached to the boom tip by means of a sliphook. If the net catches on an obstruction, the sliphook opens, releasing the towing block so that the force is transferred to the block at the stern. This arrangement allows easy recovery of the gear.

Hauling

When hauling, both nets are heaved in until they are at the boom tips (see Fig. 43) and the outriggers are then topped some 30 to 40 degrees to the horizontal. The line attached to the cod-end strap is recovered and hoisted aboard by a tackle from the cargo boom, taken to a warping head or auxiliary drum, and elevated for emptying.

Setting

When first setting the gear on arrival at the grounds, the beam trawls are hoisted on the booms which are then swung out at about 30 degrees to the horizontal; the same method is used for recovery.

All operations are undertaken while the vessel steams along a straight course.

Fig. 44. Belgian double rig trawler. This vessel is also rigged for single net stern trawling.

MID-WATER TRAWLING

The mid-water trawl is used to capture pelagic species that school at various levels between the sea bed and the surface.

While bottom trawls are often towed for several hours at a time and fish a large area, so capturing loosely distributed fish, the mid-water trawl is usually towed only some 10 to 20 minutes in order to pass through and catch a particular shoal of fish. Much of the vessel's time is spent hunting for fish in schools large enough to justify shooting the net; successful mid-water trawling requires the effective use of various electronic aids, both to find the fish and to manoeuvre the vessel while catching them; the net must be set at the correct depth, and the

vessel proceed on a course that will ensure the net passes through the school.

Due to the density of the fish schools through which the net passes, the catch per tow is much greater than for bottom trawls, perhaps by a ratio of 10:1. However, whereas the bottom trawl is towed for perhaps 18 out of 24 hours, only between 3 and 6 tows may be made with the mid-water trawl each 24 hours.

Both single vessel and pair trawling are of importance in mid-water; the latter is particularly useful in connection with smaller, low-powered vessels, and is especially applicable in shallower waters where a single vessel passing over the fish tends to scare them downwards so that they may pass below the level of the net. In addition, two-boat trawling appears to offer advantages in that the towing warps do not pass through and frighten the school of fish before the net reaches them.

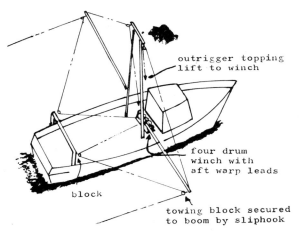

outrigger topping
lift to winch

four drum
winch with
aft warp leads

block

towing block secured
to boom by sliphook

Fig. 46. Safety arrangement aboard beam trawler. This arrangement allows the pull to be transferred to the lower aft blocks if a net hangs up while towing.

The depth at which the trawl fishes may be adjusted by varying the vessel's speed and the length of the towing warps; there may also be some changes made in the rigging of the net and gear, depending on the water depth and whether the net is fishing near the bottom or surface.

The towing speed depends on whether the species being hunted are fast or slow swimmers; for some fish, 2 to 3 knots is sufficient, while for faster swimming species, 4 to $4\frac{1}{2}$ knots is essential. It is important, therefore, that the size of the net be matched to the vessel's power to suit a particular application.

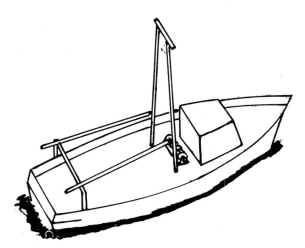

Fig. 45. Stowing the derricks aboard double rig beam trawler. The net derricks or outriggers are swung aft and supported by the low stern gantry while stowed.

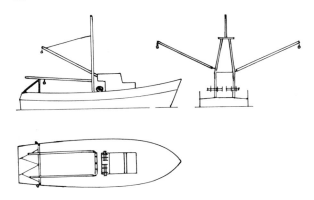

Fig. 47. Layout of European double rig trawler. This sketch shows a vessel used both for single stern trawling and double-rig beam trawling.

It is vital in this method of trawling to have a means of determining, within fine limits, the position of the net between bottom and surface; for this purpose it is usual to provide some form of instrumentation at the net which transmits the required information back to the towing vessel. Both pressure capsules and transducers similar to those used with echo sounding machines are utilized for this purpose.

Where pressure capsules are used, as on the west coast of the U.S.A., they are mounted at the doors in pods attached to the wires. In this case, the signals are transmitted to recording machines in the wheelhouse through special towing warps with conductor cables built into them. These conducting warps have the disadvantage that very large diameter blocks and deck bollards are required on the towing vessel (approx. 20 inches diameter minimum). The cost of these blocks and the cable appears excessive.

A much more common method is to attach a transducer to the centre of the headline, signals from which are transmitted through a separate, relatively light, electric cable (handled by a special winch aboard the towing vessel) to the depth-recording machine in the wheelhouse of the towing vessel (see Fig. 48, 49). Alternatively these signals may be transmitted by the transducer to be picked up by the operating vessel by a receiver either towed from a boom at one side or mounted in the hull. The readings from this transducer show the height of the headline above the sea bed, also the depth of the footrope below the headrope; the echo sounder aboard the parent vessel shows the depth of the fish school. The skipper, by using these instruments, can therefore adjust his speed and warp length ot ensure the net passes through the depth of the fish school.

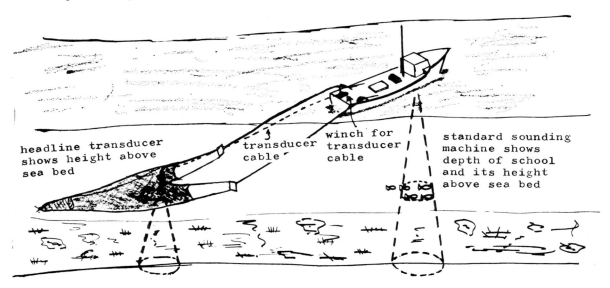

Fig. 48. One boat mid-water trawling. Although the net is similar to a cone, the operation is very much the same, and may be undertaken by vessels outfitted for bottom trawling. An additional winch is used to handle the electrical cable from the headline transducer on the net. Signals from the transducer are fed to a sounding machine aboard the vessel, and allow the net to be set to tow at the correct depth.

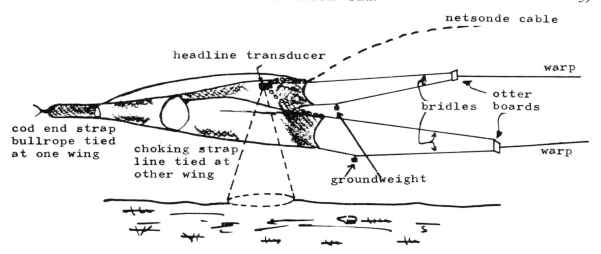

Fig. 49. One boat mid-water trawl with netsonde. A cod end strap is fitted to bring the cod end aboard for emptying. The choking strap is used to prevent the fish escaping, and for splitting. Bridles from the wings are taken to doors and warps lead to towing vessel in the usual manner. A weight is attached to each lower wire of the bridle, ahead of the wing. Floats are seized to the headline and the footrope is often weighted with chain. A headline transducer is seized to the webbing at the headline, the cable being taken around the headline to a connector at one wing; the transducer cable is plugged into this connector and led to the towing vessel.

It is common for vessels undertaking mid-water trawling to be fitted with sonar for detecting fish schools and manoeuvring the vessel when "on fish".

The Mid-Water Trawl Net

The trawl resembles more a cone of netting rather than the flat bag of the bottom trawl, the mouth taking up somewhat of an oval, circular, or square shape depending on the design.

During normal use, the net does not come into contact with the sea bed except in very shallow water, when the headline may lie on the surface while the footrope scrapes the bottom. The net is therefore of relatively light construction, enabling a vessel to tow a larger mid-water trawl than it could a bottom trawl with its heavy net and bottom gear.

There are a number of designs for mid-water nets, but generally they may be grouped into the types that have the same shape above and below, ending in small wings at either side (see Fig. 49), and the types which are essentially constructed from four panels of netting joined to form a box shape with small extension gussets or wings at each corner (see Figs. 51, 52).

Floats are placed at the headline, and the footrope is often weighted with chain; other weight and float arrangements depend on whether one or two boat trawling is being undertaken. As well as assisting the net in maintaining its correct geometry, the chain on the footrope assists in providing a strong echo on the recording machine from the headline transducer.

In addition to the cod-end strap with the bullrope fastened at one wing while towing, a second or "choking strap" is used to prevent fish from escaping while the net is being brought aboard. This passes through rings well forward of the cod-end strap. The line from the choking strap is tied at the other wing while towing.

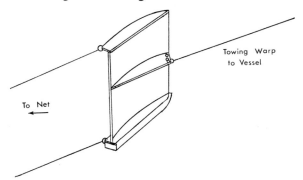

Fig. 50. "Suberkrub" type doors used in midwater trawling. Doors have curved surface, often circular; vertical dimension is greater than length to provide good hydrodynamic efficiency.

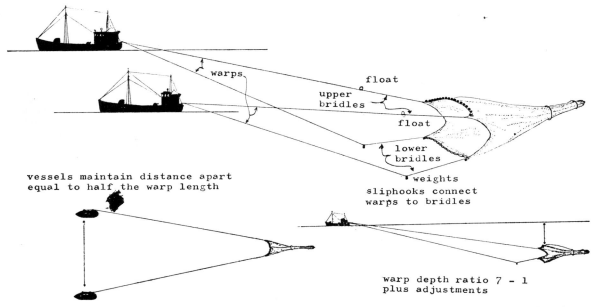

Fig. 51. Two boat mid-water trawling. Each vessel tows one side of the net using two warps connected to bridles from upper and lower wings at that side. A headline transducer is utilized, feeding to one of the towing vessels.

The headline transducer is usually set into a wood or fibreglass block clipped to the webbing at the centre of the headline; the cable if used is seized along the headline to one wing where it ends in a connector. The cable carrying the signals to the sounding machine is plugged into the connector and runs freely up to a special winch mounted aboard the parent vessel.

One Boat Mid-Water Trawling

Trawl Gear and Vessel

A common arrangement of mid-water trawl gear for one boat operation is illustrated in Figure 49. This particular sketch shows the type of net with short side wings; as an alternative, the box type of trawl (Fig. 52) is often used for single vessel operation.

A two or three bridle arrangement connects the net to the trawl doors; the usual flat design of door may be used for mid-water work, but it is common to utilize one of several designs especially built for the purpose; these may be of a double airfoil "wing" section (Cobb doors), or of a single curved surface stiffened with flat plate (Suberkrup doors). In both cases the height of the door is greater than its length (see Fig. 50). The weight is important in

ensuring the designed towing characteristics of the gear.

The usual floats are seized to the headrope and the footrope is weighted with chain. Additional floats may be used at the wing ends, and weights (often between 50 and 150 pounds) are suspended from the lower bridle to assist in maintaining the desired net geometry.

The transducer with its cable is arranged as described previously; the transducer cable winch, which may be power or hand operated depending to some extent on the vessel size, is usually sited at the towing vessel's stern.

This method can be used with any vessel arranged for bottom trawling, the hook-up of bridles, doors, warps and independent cables being rigged to suit the method of handling for which the vessel is outfitted.

Operation

The hauling, setting, and general net handling operation is similar to that for bottom trawling, depending on the manner in which the trawl gear is rigged and the net handling arrangements aboard the towing vessel. The following additional factors are important:

1. When hauling, the choking strap is tightened as soon as practicable to prevent the fish from swimming forward and escaping through the mouth.

2. When setting and hauling, the transducer cable must be run out and hauled evenly with the warps and bridles.

3. The groundweights must be lifted inboard and outboard, as the net mouth is brought aboard.

Two Boat (Pair) Mid-Water Trawling

Trawl Gear

The common arrangement of the gear for pair trawling in mid-water is illustrated in Figures 51, 52. This particular sketch shows the box type of net that is normally used for two-boat towing.

Each vessel tows one side of the net, using twin warps attached to the upper and lower bridle legs. Horizontal opening of the mouth is achieved by maintaining the correct spacing between vessels while towing. Vertical opening of the mouth is obtained by the disposition of headline floats and chain-weighted footrope. Larger floats are often attached to each headline gusset, and weights are used to achieve the correct bottom geometry of the gear. A small weight (often 56 pounds) is attached to the lower bridle just forward of the footrope gussets, and larger weights (up to 360 pounds) are

secured to the ends of the lower warps just forward of their attachment to the lower bridles.

The warps are connected to the bridles by a slip-hook arrangement to permit rapid connection and disconnection. The transducer arrangements are as described previously, except that the cable is usually taken to the vessel that hauls and sets the gear.

Vessel

Generally, any vessel outfitted for single-boat towing can be used for pair trawling, providing some simple arrangements are made.

In the case of a side trawler, a double block is usually hung from the after gallows, with leads arranged from the winch so that both warps are towed from this point (see Fig. 53). Aboard a stern trawler, a double block is hung at one gallows, usually starboard, and warp leads must be arranged to permit this.

Several light snatchblocks are also required to provide the necessary leads to the winch drums and warping heads for net hauling, their location depending on the vessel layout.

Operation of Side Trawler

The method of operation for one particular vessel arrangement is shown in Figure 53; the sequence aboard other boats is similar, depending on their deck layout.

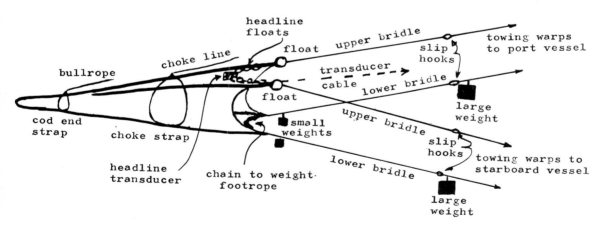

Fig. 52. Mid-water trawl rigged for two boat working. Warps from each towing vessel are connected by slip hooks to upper and lower bridles from each side of the net which is constructed of four equal panels. Large weights, e.g. 350 pounds, are suspended from the warp end at the lower bridle, and smaller weights, e.g. 56 pounds, are positioned on the bridle at the wing connection. The footrope is often weighted with chain. The headrope has floats secured along its length with larger floats at each wing end, to assist in maintaining the correct net geometry. Cable from a headline transducer, which is set in a wood block and lashed to the twine at the headrope, is seized along the headrope to a connector at one wing; the transducer cable is plugged in at this point and taken to the special winch aboard one of the towing vessels.

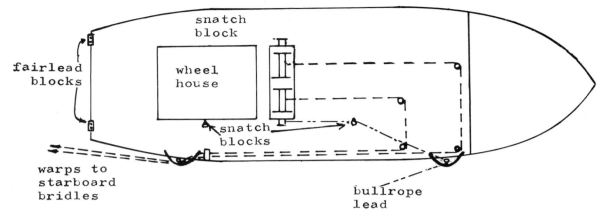

Fig. 53. Deck layout for side trawler engaged in mid-water pair trawling. Both warps pass through a double towing block at the after gallows and tow one side of the net. The other vessel tows the other side of the net, the bridles being passed from one boat to the other by messenger. The net is brought aboard at the stern when hauling, the bridles being passed through the fairlead blocks aft to the warping drums. With this arrangement, only the lower bridle will be heaved on the warping head, the upper bridle being coiled down by hand.

When towing, the warp leads are arranged as described previously; when the time comes to haul back, both vessels are slowed and the warps hauled in up to the bridles, the transducer cable being heaved evenly with the warps. At this point the large weights are left hanging on the warp ends over the gallows blocks.

The port hand vessel now attaches a messenger line to its two bridles and disconnects the warps. The vessels come together and by use of a heaving line, the messenger is passed to the starboard boat where it is placed in the port fairlead block aft, and run through suitably placed snatchblocks to the warping head. When these bridles reach deck level, heaving is continued by power and hand until the mouth of the net is heaved over the stern by hand.

When the net reaches deck level, the small weights are lifted aboard and the choker strap tightened on the warping head. The bullrope is now taken through the forward gallows block to a warping head and the main body of the net brought alongside with the cod-end forward. The catch may now be split and brought aboard in the usual manner.

When setting, the two boats take up a position side by side, the starboard vessel pays out the net astern while moving slowly ahead; at the appropriate time the mouth is placed overboard, the small weights lifted out, and the bridles paid out. With the vessels stopped the starboard bridles are attached to the towing warps and the port side bridles shackled to a messenger line which is then passed over to the portside boat where they may be connected to their warps. Both vessels now move ahead to pay out the warps and transducer cable evenly, radio contact assisting this operation.

Operation of Stern Trawler

Essentially, the operation is the same as that described for the side trawler, but at the time the bridles are both evenly located over the stern, the procedure is that normally followed for the particular vessel layout. As the net operations are handled over the stern in all cases, stern trawlers would appear to offer some advantage.

DREDGING

This method is used for harvesting shellfish from the sea bed. The towed dredge, or rake, scrapes up the complete shells from the bottom and stores them in its bag until they are brought aboard. Once aboard the operating vessel, the shells may be opened and the meat extracted, or they may be sacked for transportation to shore-based processing facilities.

For inshore, shallow waters, dredging may be carried out by small boats towing a single dredge. Important offshore fisheries exist also, such as those for scallops on the east coast of North America and Alaska. These fisheries utilize larger vessels towing two or three dredges.

Inshore Dredging

This operation is usually undertaken in relatively shallow water within short distance of the land.

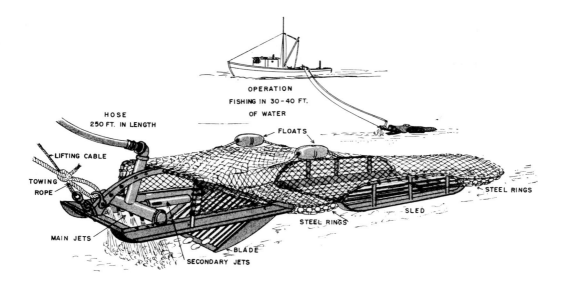

Fig. 54. Hydraulic dredging operation.

Top: water jets are used to scour shells which are then dug up by the blade to pass back into the bag. Water for jets is pumped through hose from operating vessel.

Bottom: typical vessel operating hydraulic dredge for surf clams off east coast of the United States. The dredge is shown on deck and the water pipe can be seen stowed to starboard of the towing post. When fishing, the tow rope is secured to the towing post; when setting and hauling the lifting cable runs over a block on the boom to handle the dredge.

The vessels and gear are therefore of a size and arrangement to permit easy manoeuvring under restricted conditions.

Vessels working close inshore are rarely more than 45 feet in length, while those working several miles offshore may reach 65 feet in length.

The dredge gear used depends on the type of shellfish being sought and the sea bed characteristics. If the shells may be scraped off, or are just beneath a suitable bottom, then a simple dredge may be used.

If, on the other hand, the creature is found wholly or partially buried in difficult bottom, special arrangements may be needed to extract and gather the shells. A typical example of such techniques is shown in Figure 54 where water jets using water pumped under pressure through a pipe from the

Fig. 55. Scallop dredge. The mouth frame is of steel with steel rings forming the underpart of the bag, which undergoes rough treatment when scooping up shellfish from rough bottom. Similar types of dredge may be used for other species. The width may amount to 16 ft. An 11 ft. dredge weighs approximately 1,400 lbs. when empty and up to 4,000 lbs. when full.

vessel are used to free the shells for collection by the bag.

Offshore Dredging
Gear and Vessels

A typical dredge, or rake, is shown in Figure 55. The rectangular mouth is a heavily constructed steel framework to which the towing arms and brackets are attached. The bottom bar of the mouth is formed into a knife or scythe which scrapes the bottom, freeing and lifting the shellfish which then pass into the bag. The bag is a constant width throughout its length, being held out at the rear by a steel angle or "clubstick".

The underside of the bag is usually formed of steel rings crimped together so that it can withstand rough treatment from the sea bottom and the shells. The top is usually of steel rings at the rear end where the shells gather, but further forward sash cord webbing is common.

Rakes vary in width from some 5 feet for smaller vessels up to 16 feet for vessels 100 feet in length. As an example, an 11-foot dredge when empty weighs about 1,400 pounds and perhaps 4,000 pounds when full. They are towed by a single cable of heavy plow steel wire (1-inch diameter for 16-foot rakes), shackled to the towing ring of the arms.

Vessel layouts for dredging may follow one of three configurations:

1. Two dredge operation working from the foredeck.
2. Two dredge operation working from the afterdeck.
3. Triple dredge operation working from the afterdeck.

Two Dredge Operation Working from the Foredeck

Typical vessel arrangement can be seen from Figures 56 and 57. The layout can be seen as similar to the usual side trawler; in fact, many of these vessels undertake both dredging and side trawling.

For dredging, heavy gallows frames are sited abreast the foremast and immediately abaft the forecastle; these gallows are usually heavy steel weldments arranged to pivot outboard during towing, and held in the desired position by a rack and pin arrangement. Two dredges are towed, one from each gallows frame.

Two permanently stayed booms are rigged from the foremast with blocks for dredge-handling tackles at their tips. The winch is sited forward of the deckhouse at the after end of the working deck and has either two main barrels for the towing cables plus two auxiliary barrels plus two warping heads, or it may have the simple two drum and two warping head arrangement. The tendency is toward the additional safety of the former arrangement, wires for lifting the heavy dredges being more safely handled from the auxiliary drums rather than on warping heads.

The Operation

While fishing, the gallows are pivoted outboard. While towing (see Fig. 56) the wires run from the winch drums forward round deck bollards, through sheaves at the base of the gallows and so over the gallows towing blocks.

The dredges are hauled back alternately; when the time comes, the appropriate winch drum is clutched in and the rake heaved in until it is hanging from the gallows frame (Fig. 56); at this point the tackle from the boom at that side is hooked to the dredge frame, taken to the winch, and the dredge lifted aboard, while the warp is backed off slightly. When it is on deck, the tackle is unhooked from the frame and rehooked to the clubstick at the rear of the bag, which is then hoisted up so the dredge is lifted upside down to dump the catch on the deck;

the rake is lifted outboard and the towing cables run out to commence fishing once again.

Two Dredge Operation from the After Deck

In common with most other fishing methods, many modern vessels are being designed and built that work from the after deck. Vessels built for dredging (see Fig. 58) have the winch sited abaft the forecastle and/or deckhouse, twin permanently stayed booms from the mainmast which is sited immediately abaft the winch, and twin pivoting gallows abreast the mast.

This arrangement has the advantage that the working deck is more sheltered and the movement of the vessel is less pronounced at the working area, so that the vessel can continue fishing in heavier weather than when work is taking place forward. Also, it is often possible to provide a greater length of working deck enabling larger dredges to be handled, and the scallop processing can be carried on under cover beneath the after end of the long forecastle deck.

The Operation

The operation is similar to that described for the twin-dredge arrangement using the forward working deck.

Fig. 56. 89 ft. U.S. East coast scalloper. This scalloping vessel works from the foredeck. Hinged Gallows are either side of the mast; the dredge is lifted inboard by whips from the twin booms at the foremast.

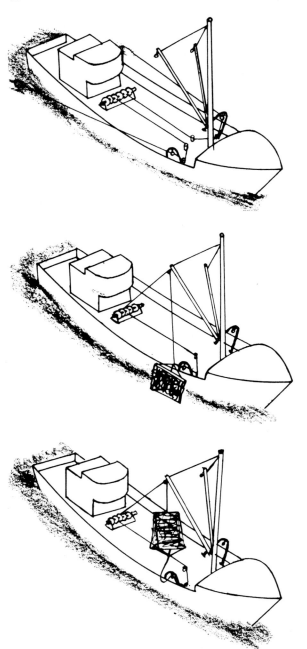

Fig. 57. Dredging operation from fore deck.

Top: towing cables run forward from winch drums round deck bollards and sheaves at base of gallows, and so over towing blocks hung from gallows, to the dredges. One dredge is towed from each side of the vessel.

Middle: hauling: the winch drum hauls towing cable until dredge towing arms are at gallows block. Whip from block at boom is taken to auxiliary drum or warping drum, is hooked to dredge frame and dredge is swung aboard. The towing cable is eased slightly to facilitate this operation.

Bottom: the whip is unhooked from the frame and hooked onto the rear angle, the clubstick, so that the dredge may be lifted and the catch fall through the mouth onto the deck. The dredge may now be swung out over the side, the towing cable run out and fishing continued.

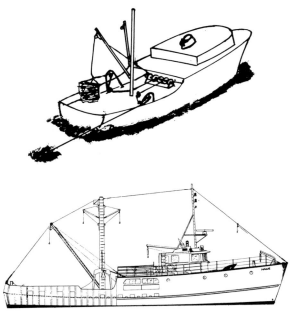

Fig. 58. Stern dredging vessels.

Top: dredging operation from after deck is similar to that from the foredeck.

Bottom: this profile drawing of a 95 ft. stern scalloper shows positions and size of gallows, mast and booms. The small derricks at the masthead are for unloading.

Triple Dredge Operation Working from the After Deck

The arrangement of the vessel and the layout of fishing gear are illustrated in Figure 59, from which it may be seen that the operation utilizes an entirely different procedure during towing and when handling the rakes.

Of particular importance is the hinged flap operated by hydraulic rams at the transom. In place of the usual gallows as towing points, the two outer rakes are towed from booms extending just beyond the ship's side, heeled to an unstayed mast placed aft; the centre dredge is towed from blocks on the mast.

When fishing, the rakes are brought aboard in turn, and one is always being handled while two are fishing. The time for heaving, emptying and setting varies, depending on the depth of water and the

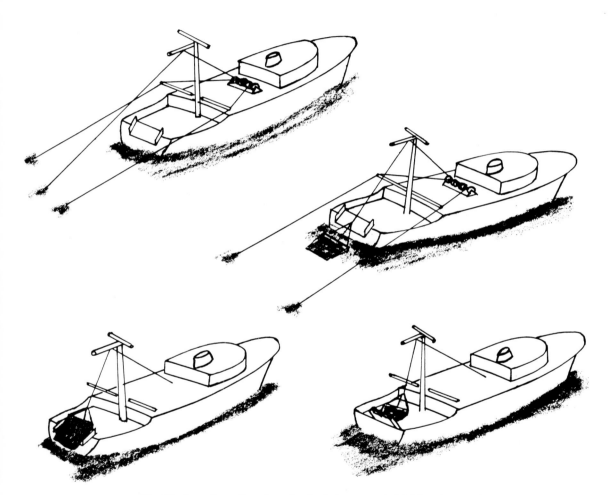

Fig. 59. Operation of semi-mechanized stern operated triple rake vessel.

Top: towing: rakes are towed from twin outrigger booms at each side of after mast, and from fore and aft outrigger at masthead.

Middle right: heaving: the stern flap is hinged downwards outboard to receive the rake which is hauled up by the towing warp.

Middle left: heaving is continued until rake lies in, and is held by stern flap.

Bottom: rake is tilted inwards to tip catch onto deck inside transom. Flap is then tilted back outboard so that the rake slides out, and towing cable run out to commence fishing.

length of cable out, but averages some 20 minutes when in 30 to 50 fathoms depth, providing no repairs are necessary. This arrangement, as might be expected, is said to increase production over the traditional two rake operation by some 50 per cent.

The Operation

When hauling back, the appropriate winch drum is clutched in and heaves up the dredge, the vessel being manoeuvred so that it comes in at the centre-line. The dredge is pulled up the stern flap (see Fig. 59) until the clubstick is caught and held by leads and chocks on the flap sides. The flap is now tilted inwards so that the contents are discharged on to the deck.

To set out the dredge, the flap is tilted outboard again and the warp run out, allowing the dredge to fall away and return to the water. This method offers the advantage that no running wires and lifting are necessary, the complete operation being handled by the towing wire and tilting flap. Also, the dredge is held tightly in position during emptying, whereas in the previously described methods it sways with the vessel's movements and presents a danger to the crew.

Encircling Gear

PURSE SEINING

PURSE seining is a method of particular importance for the capture of species utilized in bulk reduction processes, such as fish meal for animal feeds. It is also used extensively in the catching of species having high individual value, such as tuna, used as food fish.

The basic method of purse seining involves the setting out of a long net to form a wall of webbing around the school of fish being taken, the top of the net usually being in the surface. When the net has encircled the fish, its bottom is pulled together so that an artificial pond of webbing holds the catch. This pond is then gradually made smaller until the fish are gathered alongside the vessel and may be taken aboard.

For the most part, the method is utilized in harvesting pelagic species swimming from the surface to a depth of perhaps 70 fathoms. In some fisheries, however, the purse seine is used to catch demersal species, such as cod, swimming near the sea bed, and in such cases the wall of netting is sunk so that the bottom is on the sea bed with the top below the surface.

A number of different methods of net arrangements and gear handling are in common use, the one chosen for a particular application depending largely on the characteristics and behaviour of the species being harvested.

The Net

These may be divided into two general types, those in which the fish are finally contained in a bag or "bunt" at the centre of the length, and those in which the bunt is at one end (see Fig. 60). The detailed shape and rigging of the net varies widely, however, depending on the method of handling and the species.

The corkline, to which are fastened a large number of cork floats, runs along the top of the net to provide flotation, and a leadline, to which are fastened a large number of weights, runs along the net bottom to sink the webbing so that it forms the desired "wall".

Below the leadline, in most cases, a purse line runs through rings connected by short lengths of rope to the leadline; the purse line is pulled from one or both ends through the rings, in order to close up the bottom of the net. The ring net is a variation of this arrangement and will be described later.

Method of Use

Purse seining may be undertaken by either a single vessel, by a pair of vessels, or by a combination of large and auxiliary boats. The various methods will be described in turn.

Single Vessel Operation Using Purse Seine with Bunt at One End

This is probably the most common method of working a purse seine. Two distinct vessel layouts and operating techniques are in general use—the Western One Boat System, and the Icelandic or Norwegian One Boat System. The method of working was first developed on the west coast of the United States and Canada, where the common west coast vessel layout was used, and has been adapted to the needs of the Icelandic and Norwegian fisheries. A method particularly useful in some applications is Drum Seining, a variation on the general method.

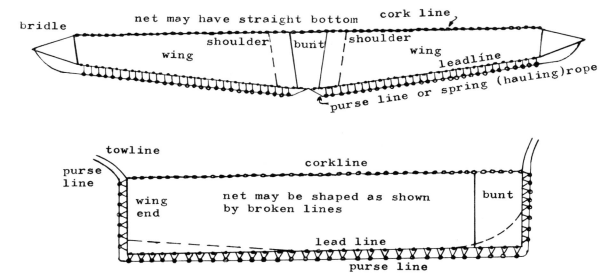

Fig. 60. Encircling nets of the purse seine type.

Top: net constructed with bag, tongue or bunt at centre to contain catch. When fish are surrounded, net is pulled aboard from both ends until only the bunt is left overside containing the catch. Net may be rectangular rather than shaped as shown.

Bottom: net constructed with bunt at one end. When the fish are surrounded the bottom of the net is drawn together and the net hauled aboard by the wing end only until fish are contained in bunt.

The Western One Boat System

Vessel and Gear

The vessel layout shows features traditional to the west coast of the United States and Canada, as may be seen from Figures 62 to 64. The deckhouse, containing some accommodation, is forward with the engine room below; forward of the engine room is a forecastle providing sleeping accommodation. The fish hold lies abaft the engine room and below the clear working deck, with a net storage space or platform aft and lazarette below. The purse seine winch is sited abaft the deckhouse and is arranged to provide athwartships leads to purse line blocks hung from a purse davit on the side from which the net is set (usually starboard).

A firmly stayed mast is situated at the after end of the deckhouse from which is hung a long boom supporting a power block (a self-powered freely swinging V-sheave) at its extremity for handling the net. Topping arrangements are provided for the boom, which also supports at least one set of falls and one whip. A lighter, shorter boom may be hung above the main boom to assist with handling the purse rings and the fish pump, or brailer, used to

bring the fish aboard from the net. A bar on which the purse rings are stored is sited on the bulwark at the side from which the net is set.

Operation

The method of working is illustrated in Figure 61. While steaming to the fishing grounds, the net is laid out on the after end of the working deck, with the bunt end at the top of the pile, so that it can be streamed out over the stern when setting. Usually, the corklines are placed one side of the deck with the leadline on the other side; the purse rings with the purse line rigged through them are placed on the storage bar.

Setting

When a school of fish is located, the vessel manoeuvres, depending on wind and tide, so that it can pay out the net and complete a circle around the fish. When setting, the bunt of the net is usually attached to a seine skiff, a heavily constructed open power boat, which is dropped into the water and assists in pulling out the net; an alternative arrangement is to drop a buoy attached to the bunt. The vessel then steams in a complete circle around the

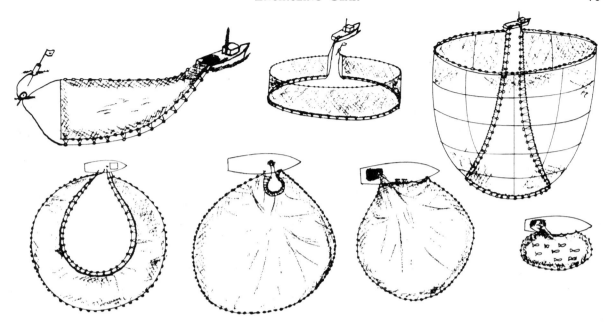

Fig. 61. Western one boat method of purse seine operation.

Top left: setting the net; vessel moves ahead, drops skiff or buoy with net attached and moves in circular path paying out net over stern.

Top centre: completing the set; the vessel has completed the circle and is about to retrieve the buoy or skiff in order to take aboard the bridle and purse line.

Top right: Ready to purse; the floatlines and purse lines have been brought aboard; each end of the purse line is taken to the purse winch and both ends pulled in together drawing the bottom of the net together.

Bottom extreme left: pursing proceeding; the bottom of the net is gradually being drawn tight.

Middle left: pursing completed; the purse rings have been pulled up and are hanging over the side. The bunt is secured forward so that the fish cannot leave the net.

Middle right: Rings aboard, web being hauled; the purse rings have been lifted aboard and the purse line removed. Net wing has been passed through power block, and the net including both floatline and leadline, also rings is being taken aboard over the power block and flaked down aft.

Extreme right: ready to remove fish. The net has been hauled until the fish are gathered close to the ships side. Brailing or pumping can now begin.

school, paying out the net (Fig. 61). Usually the net is shot over the starboard quarter while turning to starboard during the manoeuvre, but shooting to port may be carried out. If all the net is overboard before the vessel completes the circle, then the wing is towed by a tow rope fastened to it, to complete the set.

Hauling

When the vessel reaches its starting point, the purse line and net lines are regained from the skiff, or by picking up the buoy; the towline is then hauled in by the winch over a block attached to the purse davit (Fig. 62). Both ends of the purse line are now passed over the purse blocks hanging from the davit and taken to the purse winch which heaves them in

together, closing the bottom of the net (see Fig. 61). Pursing continues until the purse rings are alongside, when they are lifted aboard by means of overhead falls from the boom taken to a warping head on the winch. The purse line is now pulled through and removed from the rings either to be coiled on deck or spooled on a drum fitted for the purpose.

The net's wing is now placed in the power block and hauled aboard, corkline, twine, leadline and rings all passing over the block to the after deck where the net is stowed ready for the next set. The corkline of the net is supported by a line from the bow (see Figs. 61, 62). During the hauling operation the skiff is used to tow the vessel clear of the net and so prevent entanglement.

Hauling continues until the fish are gathered in

Fig. 62. One boat purse seining from the after deck.

Top: purse seine stacked on after deck platform. The cork line and lead lines are stacked clear of one another. The channel bar chock at the transom is for locating the skiff when it is aboard or being handled.

Bottom left: pursing; the two ends of the purse line are taken over blocks on the seine davit to the winch warping heads.

Bottom right: hauling in the web by power block; pursing has been completed and the rings lifted aboard (shown by the gather of twine just abaft the deckhouse). The net is now being hauled through the power block and flaked down aft. The corkline floats show the shape of the net. Note the net is lashed forward to assist in supporting the weight of the catch. Often, the skiff will be used to assist in supporting the corkline when the net has been dried up.

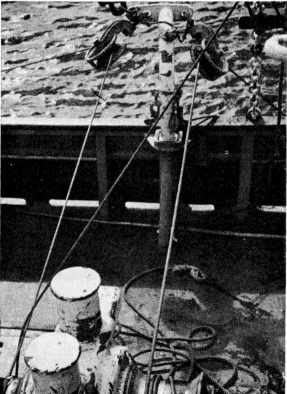

the remaining portion of the net close to the ship's side. The catch is removed from the net either by means of a fish pump lowered into the bunt of the net alongside, or by brailing. In the case of fish destined for reduction, which are usually of quite small size, such as herring, anchovy or menhaden, a centrifugal pump raises fish and water along a rubber hose to a de-watering screen alongside the hatch, from where the fish are passed into the hold and the water overboard. An electrical attraction system may be used to gather the fish in the bunt for pumping.

If pumping is impracticable due either to the size of the fish or if damage might occur to fish destined for use as food fish, such as tuna, brailing is used to transfer the catch from the net to the hold.

The brailer is a large scoop net handled by overhead falls from the boom taken to a warping head or a specially arranged drum on the winch. At the bottom of the brailer bag, rings are fitted with a line running through them so that it may be pulled together for scooping and holding fish, but opened by releasing the line, for dumping. Figure 69 shows this operation.

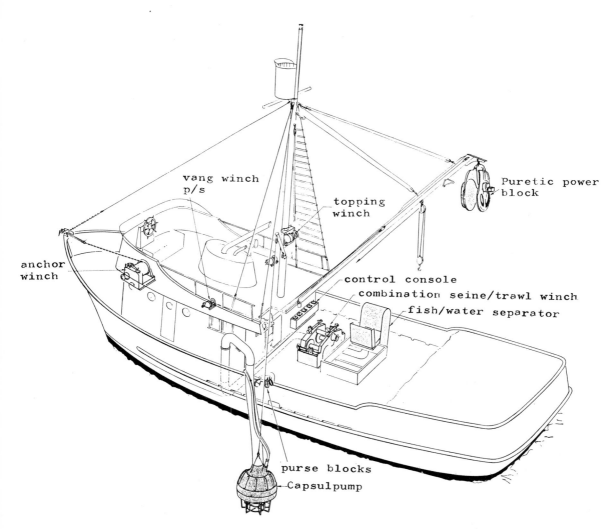

Fig. 63. Layout of small purse seiner. Note the arrangement of the fish pump and dewatering screen through which the fish pass before going into the hold.

Equipment

Winch—sited to provide athwartship leads to one side of the vessel. May be of a simple capstan or warping head type, in which case two heads would be used for hauling purse lines and a third head for handling the towline (see Fig. 62). If this type of winch is used, it is useful to provide either hand, or, more usually, powered spools to hold the lines as they come off the warping heads, and so make hand coiling unnecessary.

An alternative arrangement (see Figs. 63, 64) of particular application to larger vessels using heavier gear, is to utilize winches akin to those used for trawling, mounted so that the two ends of the purse line can be wound on to separate drums as they are brought in; after pursing is completed, the purse line is wound off one of the drums so that it is con-

tained entirely on one drum ready for setting. With this arrangement, a third drum may be fitted for handling the towline, which is wound and stored directly on this drum. Twin warping heads should be available for general line, falls, and whip handling. A special drum for brailing may be fitted, or the operation may be undertaken using a warping head.

Purse blocks and davit—(see Fig. 62) twin open sided blocks hung on a single davit, normally portable, fitted into mountings at the bulwark on the working side of the vessel. The purse davit will usually support a snatchblock for towline handling in addition to the purse blocks.

Purse ring stowage—an open ended bar or trough of sufficient length to store all purse rings, and located so that the rings can slide off astern during setting.

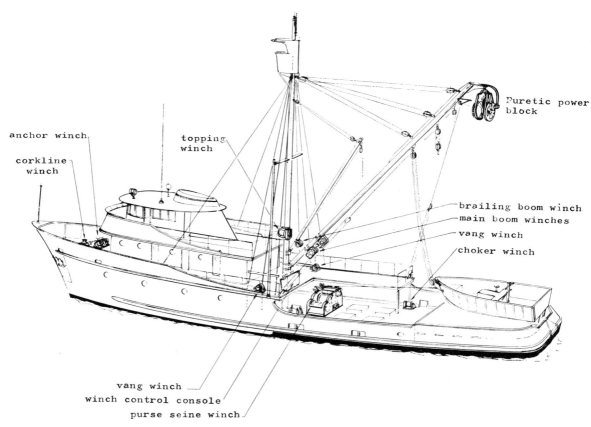

anchor winch

corkline winch

topping winch

Puretic power block

brailing boom winch
main boom winches
vang winch
choker winch

vang winch
winch control console
purse seine winch

Fig. 64. Tuna purse seiner. Shows the layout and equipment found aboard larger vessels used for extensive trips. Whereas seiners working on smaller species such as herring or anchovy can use fish pumps to advantage, vessels working tuna and other large fish, utilize brailing.

Power block—of sufficient size and power to handle the purse seine being used. It must be possible to pass bunched-up twine, corks, weights and rings through the sheave during the hauling operation. The block must be freely pivoting and self-powered, usually by hydraulics, or alternatively by a rope drive from the main winch.

Fish pump—used for industrial fish, requires sufficient length of hose to be lowered over side to bottom and extent of net; handled from overhead boom falls.

In either case, a de-watering screen may be sited alongside the hatch so that water is directed overboard, while the fish are directed into the hold. An alternative is to make provision for water drainage from the holds, which are then constructed as tanks, to a well from which it may be pumped overboard.

The Seine Skiff

The size and power of the skiff is dependent on the size of the net, together with the size and power of the purse seiner. For vessels coming within the range considered (up to some 100 feet overall), a skiff of some 16 to 18 feet in length powered with a 100 to 180 h.p. engine might be appropriate. The skiff is often constructed quite crudely of steel, and has the screw well protected by a basket guard. Primary need of the skiff is to be capable of towing the vessel, and perhaps also the net, to prevent entanglement or to clear obstacles.

Drum Seining

The general method is similar to that described when the power block is utilized. These vessels are characterized by the large drum mounted at the stern

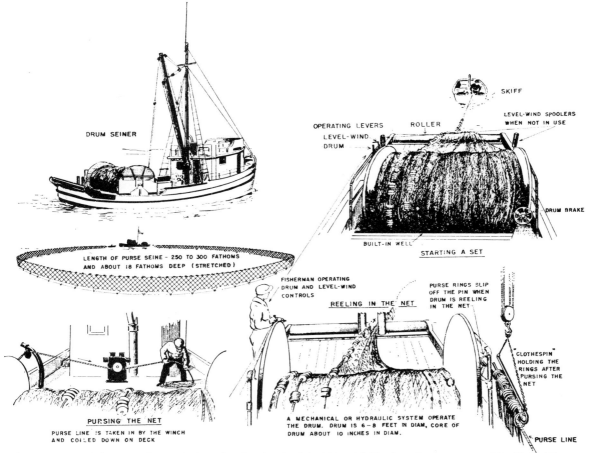

Fig. 65. Drum seining operation as depicted in Circular 48 of the N.M.F.S. Used on the west coast of the United States, this method is particularly efficient in handling shallower purse seines.

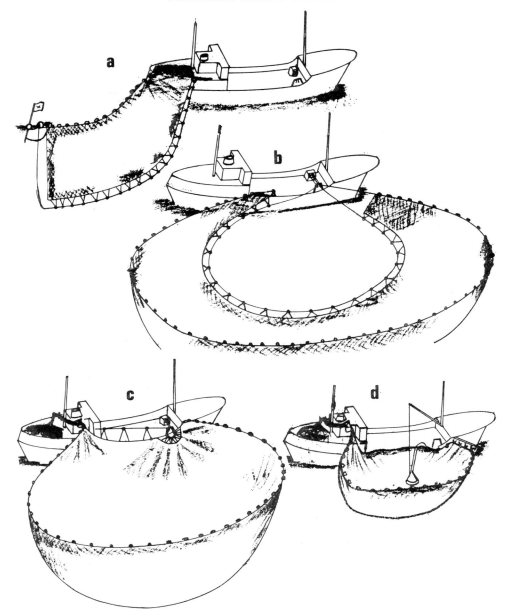

Fig. 66. European Purse Seining Operation.

(a) setting; net is set from after deck, rings being stowed on bar forward of stacked net.

(b) pursing; when the buoys have been retrieved, pursing is carried out by a winch situated on foredeck. Capstan on foredeck is used to haul over-run (tow) line.

(c) hauling; pursing complete, the net is passed over power block hung from crane at after house and thence over transporter block to stacking position. Rings (of clip-on type) are passed from pursing davit forward to power block along wire.

(d) pumping; the bunt is held open by boom from forecastle deck and the pump handled by boom from foremast.

(Fig. 65). When on board, the net is stored on the drum, and when setting it is paid out from the drum over the stern in the usual manner. Pursing is performed by a winch abaft the deckhouse, but the net is hauled round a spooling device at the stern on to the drum where it is stored until shot away again. Figure 65 illustrates these operations.

The drum has proved particularly successful in handling relatively shallow nets.

The Icelandic/Norwegian System

Vessel and Gear

The basic principles of the purse seine operation is similar to the Western one boat arrangement, utilizing both purse winch and power block (or in larger vessels a net winch). The vessels, however, show a widely differing layout, being constructed along the lines of the traditional longliner used in the fisheries of northern Europe and Iceland.

A typical vessel layout is shown in Figures 66 and 67. The working deck is situated abaft a high forecastle or whaleback which provides protection from the seas, and forward of a poop or deckhouse structure with wheelhouse above. The purse winch is sited at the forward end of the working deck with athwartship leads to purse blocks mounted on a davit or gallows at the working side (usually starboard). The purse seine net is stored and set from the starboard side of the poop deck aft, a special steel bulwark being arranged to contain it.

For hauling, a power block may be hung on a powered crane supported from the starboard side of the wheelhouse, or alternatively a powered roller type of net winch may be used; this latter equipment is especially applicable to larger vessels using heavier gear. Very often a second powered roller or "transporter" will be arranged at the after mast, to transport the net to its stacking position on the quarter as it is pulled in by the power block or net winch.

The bunt of the net when dried up alongside is supported by a boom extending outboard from the forecastle while pumping or brailing is carried on.

A seine skiff is often considered unnecessary; the net is set using a buoy, and side thruster units at the bow and stern are utilized to maintain the vessel clear of the net while hauling. Vessels without thruster units rarely use the skiff for towing clear, but may well have one aboard.

Operation

Figure 66 illustrates the purse seining operation using this system. While steaming, the net is stacked at the starboard quarter; the purse rings are placed on a storage bar, so that they slip off when setting, with the purse line rigged through them and running forward through a purse block at the davit to one barrel of the purse winch. On top of the net is a buoy having two lines attached, one a continuation of the upper edge of the net, the other the bunt end of the purse line. The latter has a float attached to take the main weight of the purse line off the buoy, so making for easier retrieval when shooting is completed.

Setting

The buoy and float are put overboard and the net is paid out over the starboard quarter while the vessel completes a circle, turning to starboard, around the fish school (Fig. 66a). It is usual to shoot the whole net plus a large length of rope fastened to the wing end, and the purse line.

Hauling

On completing the set, the buoy is retrieved, this end of the purse line unshackled and reshackled to a lead from the purse winch drum running through a purse block (Fig. 66b). Pursing is now carried out until the rings are gathered at the purse gallows. The ropes fastened to the wing end are hauled in simultaneously either by an additional lead from the purse winch or more usually by a separate vertical capstan winch.

When pursing is complete, the ropes and wing end of the net are taken through the power block (Figs. 66c, 68), which then hauls the net continuously until drying-up is sufficient for brailing or pumping. As hauling progresses, the purse rings are unclipped from the purse line at the gallows and reclipped to a wire rigged so that they can slide aft until they are again unclipped to be passed through the power block and stowed (Fig. 66c).

The bunt end of the net is hooked to a boom, mounted at the after end of the forecastle, to assist in providing a "pond effect" of the bunt, and brailing or pumping is now undertaken as described previously, see Figures 66d, 69.

Equipment

The equipment required is very similar to that for the Western one boat system.

Purse winch—sited to provide leads to purse blocks hung from gallows or davit at forward end of working deck. A two drum winch having storage capacity or a twin barrel warping head type is suitable, in the latter case separate storage drums being useful. Either an additional head or a separate capstan type winch is required for handling net lines.

In addition to the ring storage bar aft, a wire should be rigged from the purse gallows to a point adjacent to the power block for transporting the purse rings aft as necessary during the hauling operation.

Power block—hung from powered crane at forward end of net storage area aft; it is convenient to support the crane from the wheelhouse structure. In addition, a powered transporter barrel to carry the net to the required location for stacking should be fitted. This is usually and conveniently hung from the after mast. As an alternative to the power block, a net winch (see Fig. 68) may be fitted.

For handling catch—a fish pump or brailer with de-watering screens, etc., is necessary.

Vessel Manoeuvring

Side thrust units at bow and stern, or alternatively a seine skiff are necessary to prevent entanglement of the vessel in the net while hauling.

Operation of Purse Seine Having Centre Bunt

Several distinct methods of working this arrangement of purse seine are in common use.

(a) The use of twin purse boats together with a mother ship, as used in the U.S. east coast menhaden fishery.

(b) One vessel operation, typified by the South African pursed lampara net.

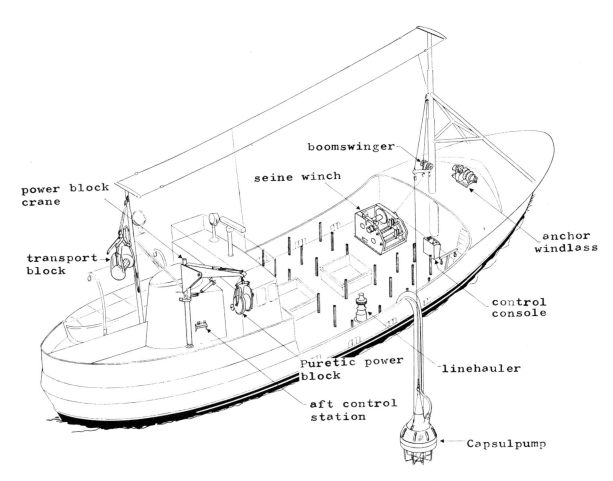

Fig. 67. Layout of Norwegian/Icelandic type herring purse seiner.

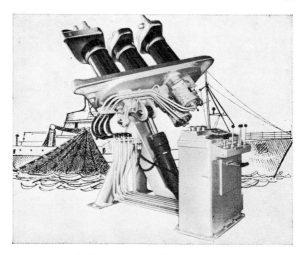

Fig. 68. Net hauling arrangements with European method of purse seining.
Left: power block mounted on crane from after house is used to haul web and for stacking net on boat deck.
Right: use of net winch. This equipment is widely used aboard larger vessels in association with a transporter roller to
   carry the net to its stacking position.

Fig. 69. Brailing mackerel aboard a Norwegian purse seiner. The brailer is handled by a lead from the overhead boom
taken to the winch located immediately abaft the forecastle. Bunt of the net is held up by the outboard boom. Purse
davit and blocks are shown.

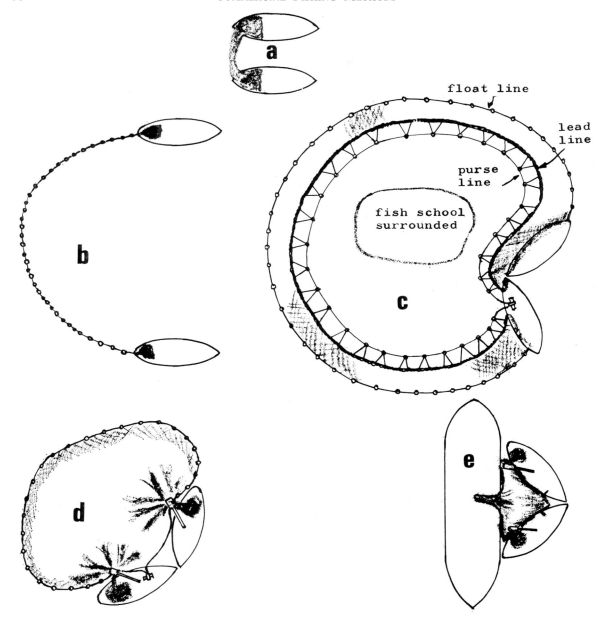

Fig. 70. Two boat and mothership method of purse seining.
(a) Two boats, each carrying half of net with centre lying between them leave mothership and steam in direction of fish school.
(b) Boats separate and surround school, each paying out net including float line, lead line and purse line.
(c) School is surrounded, one boat passes its purse line to the other which then purses net by winch having twin warping heads for the purpose. Before pursing, a heavy weight (ton weight) may be dropped down purse line from each boat to hold down lead line and purse line so that latter is pulled in horizontally.
(d) Using power blocks, webbing is pulled aboard at each end, half aboard each purse boat.
(e) When web is hauled up, so that fish are contained in centre bunt section of net, mothership comes alongside and straps net to "dry up" fish, then pumps or bails catch from net.

(c) Two vessel operation using the ring net, a variation on the common purse seine, as employed in the Scottish herring fishery.

(a) Twin Purse Boat and Mother Ship Operation

This system has been developed during use in the menhaden fishery on the east coast of the United States, and is illustrated in Figure 70.

Two seine boats, each of some 36 feet in length, are carried to the fishing grounds in davits aboard a larger mother ship. When ready to set round a school of fish, the seine boats are lowered, each carrying half the net with the centre section or bunt slung between them (Fig. 71a), and running together. On reaching the school, the boats separate, going in opposite directions to surround the fish, each paying out the net evenly including the floatline (corkline), leadline and purse line (Fig. 70b), until they come together 180 degrees from the starting point. Each boat slides a heavy weight, known as a "Tom weight" down its end of the purse line before one passes its end of the line to the other boat. Both ends of the purse line are then placed over purse blocks hung from a special davit in the pursing boat, and taken to the two warping heads of the pursing winch; both ends of the purse line are then hauled in together on this winch to purse the net (see Fig. 70). The Tom weights hold down the bottom of the net while pursing is undertaken so that, as far as possible, it is pulled together horizontally.

When pursing is completed, the rings are alongside and are then lifted aboard together with the Tom weights. Each boat then pulls in its wing; this is done by passing the webbing over a power block (see Fig. 71) mounted on a crane in each of the boats. For this operation, the purse line is split at the centre and pulled out through the rings; the webbing, as it comes in over the power block is laid out in the stern ready for the next set. Both floatline and leadline are passed through the power block together with the twine of the net and the purse rings (Figs. 70d, 71).

When the web is hauled up so that the fish are contained in the centre bag, the mother ship takes up position along the outer edge of the corkline (Fig. 70e); at this point the net will still not have been hauled in sufficiently to concentrate the fish for efficient removal. The mother ship therefore straps the net and hauls it up to dry up the catch; this operation is undertaken by using the overhead falls taken to a winch positioned for the purpose (see Fig. 71). The fish are now taken aboard the

mother ship either by a hydraulic fish pump or by brailing.

Equipment

The seine boat—It is important that these be light and provide stable working platforms. They are commonly constructed of aluminium and have typical dimensions of 36 feet length by 8·75 feet beam. As the net is stored and set over the stern, the engine is placed forward with the shaft tunnel running the length of the boat.

For hauling the net—a power block and crane sited amidships and to one side; the crane is usually hydraulically operated to pivot through 360 degrees and allow topping, with the hydraulic power block hung from the jib (see Fig. 71).

For pursing—A purse winch, either hydraulic or mechanically driven from the engine, is sited abaft the crane and consists of two warping heads. Two open blocks are hung from the davit which slots into the gunwhale. A bar or ring tray for storing purse rings is sited between purse winch and crane mounting. Drums on which the purse line may be stored while not rigged through the rings should be arranged.

Aboard mother ship—davits sited to port and starboard aft, equipped with power operated falls, to handle seine boats. Two overhead falls from boom taken to double drum winch (normally 3 ton capacity) are necessary for net strapping operation. A fish pump which can be slung outboard by use of falls from boom, with necessary de-watering facilities, is required for bringing the fish aboard.

Crew—normally 6 crew are required in each purse boat and three aboard the mother ship, making a total of 15 men to be berthed aboard the mother ship.

(b) One Boat Operation, the Pursed Lampara Seine

This method of working is used in a number of the world's fisheries, and provides an effective operation for certain species, using smaller vessels; the pilchard and mackerel fisheries of South Africa are good examples.

Vessel and Gear

The corkline length of the net is often around 1000 feet and the net itself is shaped as illustrated in Figure 60a, the purse lines being shackled to the centre point of the tongue or bunt and passing through purse rings along the bottom of each wing.

Vessels using the method are often arranged as illustrated in Figure 72, having the deckhouse and engine room aft, with the hold beneath a working deck forward of the wheelhouse. A purse winch is provided at the after end of the working deck with athwartship leads to twin rollers at the rail for pursing. Two power blocks are used, one hung from a boom at the main mast aft, the other supported similarly at the foremast. A small skiff often some 14 to 16 feet long is used to assist in setting and in floating the upper edge of the bunt when hauling.

Operation

Before setting, the net is stacked along the vessel's starboard side. The wing to be set out first (the front wing) is stacked aft, wing end on top, with the bunt and other wing coiled progressively forward along the deck edge, the back wing being coiled on the starboard foredeck. The purse line of the front wing is made fast to the skiff and that of the back wing secured forward, often at the foremast.

When setting, the skiff assists in pulling out the net while the vessel circles the school turning to starboard (Fig. 72a) until encirclement is complete, when the man in the skiff returns the purse line by use of a heaving line, to the vessel (Fig. 72b). The two ends of the purse line are passed over a roller on the gunwhale (Fig. 72c) to the winch heads, and hauling commences. At this point, the skiff proceeds to the corkline and secures at the bunt in order to prevent the net sinking from excessive weight of fish. Empty drums or other floats may also be used to assist in this.

The hauling procedure varies from that of the methods described previously; the wings are passed over the twin power blocks and both wings are hauled in simultaneously by the power blocks and purse winch together to draw the tongue to the vessel's side, rather than first pursing and then hauling the wings (Fig. 72d). As the tongue is brought nearer the surface, and when the purse lines are coming in parallel, the tongue is brought alongside, the purse winch stopped, and the tongue

secured; the leadlines are then brought aboard and the wings heaved in further (Fig. 72e), so forming the usual artificial pond alongside, and drying up the catch so the fish are contained in the bag and perhaps inner portions of the shoulders. The catch may now be brought aboard in the usual manner.

Equipment

The equipment used coincides closely with that for other methods of purse seining except that two power blocks are required.

Vessel Size

While perhaps the minimum size of vessel to use this method would be around 50 feet in length in order to provide adequate fore and aft spacing of the power blocks and space for net stowage, an average size appears to lie around 55 feet overall length.

(c) Two Vessel Operation Using the Ring Net

While ring netting is somewhat similar to the operation of the Lampara seine, the net is rectangular rather than tapered, and varies from the usual purse seines both by being lighter in structure and more particularly by the manner in which it is rigged.

In place of a purse line running through purse rings connected by lengths of rope (stoppers) to the leadline, the ring net is fitted with the stoppers spliced into a "spring" or "hauling" rope which runs beneath the leadline.

A common size of ring net is about 1000 feet in length, stretched, to be operated by two vessels in partnership. Commonly, vessels undertaking ring netting are of the M.F.V. type having the wheelhouse aft; a twin warping head winch is mounted at the after end of the working deck or around amidships, to permit athwartship leads.

Operation

The operation of ring netting is illustrated in Figure 73. One boat undertakes both setting and

---

Fig. 71. Two boat purse seine operation.

Top: Two 36 feet aluminium boats each carrying half the net steam to the school of fish before separating. Note the power blocks carried on cranes. The purse davits can be seen forward together with the pursing winches.

Middle left: the web being pulled aboard by power block. Purse winch is visible in left foreground.

Middle right: strapping operation by mothership. The net is lifted by twin overhead falls taken to a 3-ton winch sited for the purpose.

Bottom: shows layout of 36 feet by 8 feet 9 inches seine boats. Engine is forward, hydraulic crane amidships with power block; the bar for stowing purse rings can be seen abaft the crane mounting with the spool for the purse lines. Hauling has been completed and the cranes have been swung out of the way before the pump is lowered.

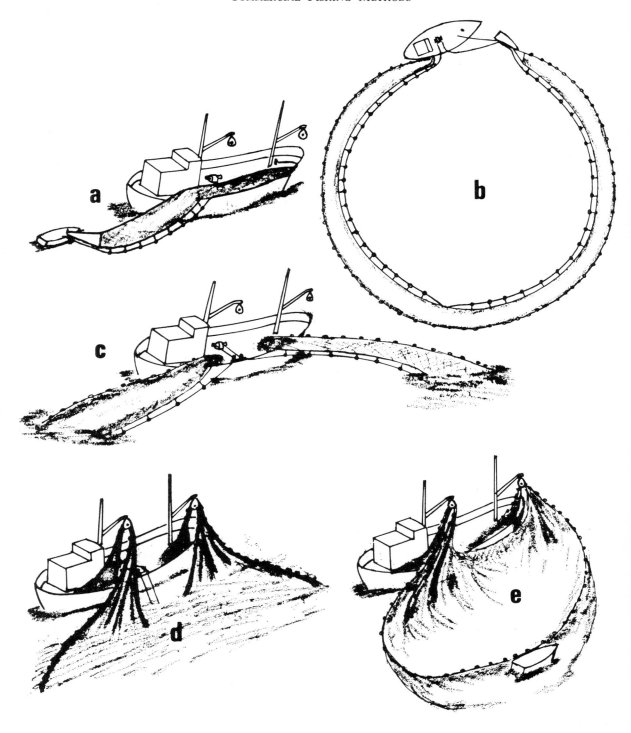

hauling operations; when preparing to set the net is stacked along one side of the vessel in a similar manner to the Lampara method.

To begin the set, the boat drops a buoy fastened to the bridle at the front wing, and then pays out the net from aft, while turning around the school of fish (Fig. 73a); at intervals, supporting buoys fastened to the corkline are dropped to assist with floatation, and the whole net is shot while the vessel completes a semicircle. By this time, the second vessel has moved to the first buoy, picked it up, and secured that end of the net for towing. Both boats together now tow the net to complete encirclement of the fish school (Fig. 73b).

The second vessel now passes its bridle and hauling rope to the setting boat, together with most of its crew who will assist with the net handling. On completing the crew transfer, the second boat takes up position (Fig. 73c) and passes a tow rope aboard the setting vessel.

The setting vessel's crew, with the assistance of the additional men who have been passed aboard, now pull both wings of the net aboard, one forward aud one aft. During this operation, the hauling rope or "spring" attached to the leadline and which bears the main weight of the net, is hauled by the twin warping heads of the ring net winch, the twine being manhandled. While the net is being hauled, the second vessel tows the first sideways to ensure it does not become entangled with the net (Fig. 73d).

When hauling is complete, with the bunt alongside, the second vessel retrieves the tow rope and steams round to the outer edge of the corkline to provide additional support, and to assist in transferring the catch (Fig. 73e).

While pumping or brailing is taking place, the vessels maintain their relative positions by the use of spring lines connecting their bows and sterns.

Equipment

Equipment required for this operation is minimal, consisting of a winch having twin warping heads,

and the usual arrangement of boom and falls from both fore and main masts to assist with the net, pump and brailer handling.

Size of Vessel

The simplicity of the operation, and the fact that the combined capacities of both vessels are available to transport the catch, means that vessels of 35 feet can operate satisfactorily, but the more usual size appears to lie between 55 feet and 75 feet overall.

SEINE NETTING

Seine netting, a bottom fishing method, is of particular importance in the harvesting of demersal species, and provides a high quality food fish product; being a combination of encirclement and dragging, it could be included under either heading.

The basic method is shown in Figure 74; long warps are laid out to surround an area of the sea bed, with a net (shaped similarly to a trawl) placed at mid-length. The two free ends of the warps are hauled in so that they close together, herding fish inwards and into the path of the net to be scooped up and brought aboard the operating vessel.

Fishing action is partly due to the movement of the warps across the sea bed, which disturbs and guides the fish within the area being worked. The effectiveness is increased on a soft bottom by the sand or mud cloud resulting from the warps' movement over the bottom.

Several different ways of working the gear are in common use, depending on the particular application in terms of species being fished, vessel characteristics, and grounds. The method is particularly suitable for vessels between 50 and 70 feet in length having low engine power, although in some areas much larger vessels make effective use of the technique.

The Net

The nets are very similar to those used in trawling but much larger and lighter, and as with otter trawl

Fig. 72. One boat operation. Hauling both wings, fish contained in bag or tongue at centre of net.
(a) Setting; the net and purse lines are secured to the skiff; the vessel then steams round the school turning to starboard and paying out the net which is laid out along the starboard side of the deck.
(b) Setting completed; the skiff passes the purse line and wing end of the net aboard. It then steams to the bag or "tongue" of the net to assist in supporting the corkline.
(c) The wing ends are now aboard and the purse lines have been taken over rollers at the bulwark to the purse winch.
(d) Hauling; the wings are passed over power blocks which then haul and stack them forward and aft while the winch pulls in the purse lines.
(e) Hauling completed; ready for removing fish. The net has been pursed so that the tongue is alongside and aboard, while the wings have been stacked along the starboard side of the deck. The skiff supports the corkline and all is ready for the fish to be brailed or pumped from the bag.

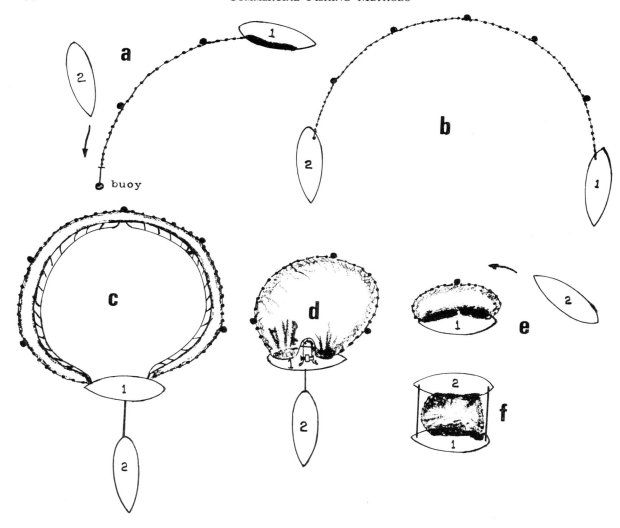

Fig. 73. Two boat operation using net with spring or hauling rope (ring net).

(a) Boat no. 1 drops buoy and circles, paying out net from stern; buoys to support net are dropped at intervals. Boat no. 2 moves to first buoy and secures bridle for towing.

(b) Boat 1 has completed paying out net which now forms half circle. Boat 2 has picked up buoy and secured bridle. Both boats together tow net around fish school.

(c) Boats have come together, encircling school. Boat 2 passes its bridle and hauling rope to boat 1, and then steams to pass tow line to boat 1. Crew may also be transferred from boat 2 to boat 1 to assist in hauling operation.

(d) Boat 1 pulls net aboard, one wing forward and one aft. At the same time, the hauling rope is pulled aboard by power winch. Boat 2 tows boat 1 clear of the net while hauling.

(e) Boat 1 has now completed hauling and fish are gathered in bag of net. Boat 2 returns tow rope and steams round to lift crew and assist in brailing or pumping catch.

(f) Boats are held together with ropes while boat 2 supports outer edge of corkline. Brailing or pumping in progress.

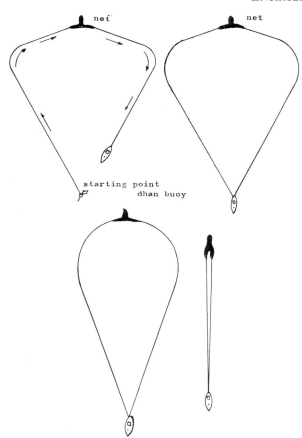

The Warps

The warps used to set out the gear are made up of a number of 120-fathom coils of manila or a specially constructed synthetic rope having a lead core to ensure that it sinks.

Commonly, a "fleet" of ten coils of rope is available for setting on each side of the net, but in order to allow the vessel to set out a less amount, if required for a particular set, only the five coils adjacent to the wings each side are spliced into a single warp, the remainder being added, as required, by G link connectors (see Fig. 75).

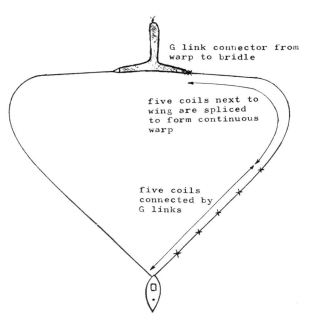

Fig. 74. Seine netting. The vessel sets out long lengths of warp, with a net at mid-length, to encircle an area of the sea bed. The warps are then hauled in progressively herding the fish inwards until they may be scooped up by the net and brought aboard.

Top left: vessel steams, paying out half the warp, followed by the net and then the remaining warp.

Top right: finish of the set; ready to haul.

Bottom left: hauling is part completed, closing the warps and herding fish into path of net.

Bottom right: the net is closed, capturing the fish.

Fig. 75. Arrangement of warps for seine netting. The five coils of rope adjacent to wing ends are spliced to form a single warp. Further coils are attached as necessary by G link connectors.

nets, they vary in design and rigging depending on the species and bottom being fished. Floats are used to elevate the headline, the groundrope is weighted and the wings are held in shape by a dan-leno arrangement or by a pole or ring held vertical by the combined effort of a float and weight. The bridle from top and bottom of the dan-leno is terminated by a swivel and G-link. A bullrope is fitted as with a trawl for handling the cod-end. For successful operation, it is of utmost importance that the nets are correctly hung and balanced.

Vessels

A layout with wheelhouse and engine forward or aft may be used. Vessels having an after wheelhouse are often flush decked, or may have a whaleback forward. The house width must be relatively small to allow clearance both for working the warps and net, and for installation of deck pounds for holding the dumped catch on either side. A clear after deck is necessary to allow gear handling. Figures 76 and 79 show the deck layout. It may be seen that a double warping barrel winch is sited forward with a rope coiler attached and extending aft.

With the wheelhouse and engine forward layout, winch and coiler are mounted just abaft the deckhouse, the net being worked over the stern; deck pounds are fitted in the usual manner for this type of vessel (see Fig. 81).

Operation

Two operating variations of the same general procedure are in common use, that chosen depending on the type of fishing and the area in which the vessel is working:

1. Fly dragging (Scottish seining) and Tow dragging (Japanese style).
2. Anchor dragging (Danish seining).

Fly Dragging (Scottish Seining)

This method is especially suitable for the capture of both flatfish and demersal round fish. It originated in Scotland (hence the term Scottish seining) as an improvement to the technique of anchor dragging which is described in the following section. Fly dragging is applicable to areas where good fishing bottom is broken up with areas of hard and rough bottom, as with the aid of precise navigational systems used in modern fisheries these may be avoided.

Although the same general technique is used both for vessels with forward and after houses, detailed procedures vary.

Engine and House Aft

When ready to begin a set the gear is laid out as shown in Figures 76 and 78. Half the total length of warp to be used is laid in coils along each side of the deck, forward of the wheelhouse, with a dhan (marker) buoy attached to the free end of the warp which is to be laid first. Either the port or starboard warp may be used to commence the operation, the choice depending on the prevailing conditions. The net is laid out on a platform aft with the warps attached. The setting procedure is illustrated in Figure 74, which shows the gear being set to starboard, i.e., the starboard warp set out first (starboard shot).

Fig. 76. Seine net vessel. Wheelhouse aft arrangement, showing layout. Winch and coiler are sited abaft foremast. When preparing to set gear, warps are laid out in coils each side of the deck. Boom aft on starboard side is used to bring cod end aboard. Towing block may be seen aft to right of crew man. Roller for setting out warps can be seen amidships at port rail in front of centre crew man.

The dhan buoy made fast to the forward end of the starboard warp is thrown overboard and the vessel steams along the desired course paying out the coils round a vertical roller set above the rail amidships (see Fig. 74). When between a half and two-thirds of the warp is out, a slow turn is made varying between 90 and 120 degrees, and the remainder of the starboard warp set out. At this point, the vessel is slowed and the net put overboard, followed by the beginning of the port warp. Picking up speed again, the vessel lays out the port warp as shown until brought to a halt alongside the dhan at the starting point.

The dhan buoy is lifted aboard, and the free ends of both port and starboard warps are placed through the rollers of the towing block set in the rail aft. From the towing block, the warps are taken together around fairlead rollers at the forward end of the deckhouse, then separated to be taken over further roller fairleads to the barrels of the winch and through the coiler (see Figs. 79, 77). If the set has been made to starboard then the towing block will be placed at the starboard side of stern, and the starboard run of warps shown in Figure 79 will be used. The fairleads immediately abaft the winch are arranged so that they may be moved athwartships (usually by about one diameter) to the correct positions for either port or starboard tows.

With the ends of both warps secure in the winch, towing commences. The vessel tows ahead at between 2 and 3 knots, depending on tide conditions, and the winch is set to pull in the warps at around 50 feet per minute. The coiler draws the ropes from the winch and coils them automatically, a crewman stacking the coils along the side deck as each is completed so that they are positioned for the next set.

When the first coil is aboard, the winch is speeded up to around 60 to 80 feet per minute and then to 80 to 100 feet per minute for the third coil. At this point in the operation, the net is usually closed (see Fig. 74) and the winch rate is then increased to between 250 to 300 feet per minute until it is stopped when the net is close aboard.

The net is now brought aboard either by hand, or by means of a power block supported by a boom off the after mast or the deckhouse (Fig. 80). When a power block is used, the warps are laid in it and both wings brought in together. As they come over the block, they are separated, one wing being flaked

Fig. 77. Winch and coiler. The coiler is mounted on the after side of the two barrel winch and coils the warps as they come off the winch barrels. Fairleads in foreground are moved athwartships to suitable positions for towing on port or starboard side.

down ready for the next set and the other piled on deck so that it may be laid on top of the net later. The complete net is brought up in this manner until the cod-end can be handled. A bullrope allows the bag to be brought alongside and lifted aboard by falls from a boom at the after end of the deckhouse (see Fig. 78).

The fish are emptied into a deck pound abreast the wheelhouse, and the net laid out on the net platform at the stern for the next set.

Engine and Wheelhouse Forward

In general, the procedure is similar to that described previously, but the gear handling is somewhat simplified by the clear after deck.

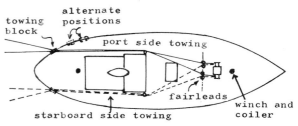

Fig. 79. Warp leads for seine net vessel with wheelhouse aft. Fairleads abaft winch are mounted so that they may be moved athwartships on a bar to required positions for port or starboard towing. The towing block may be moved to one of several locations to suit prevailing conditions.

During hauling, the warps are taken through the towing block at the stern and led directly to the winch barrels as shown in Figure 81; the coils are laid out each side of the wheelhouse (Fig. 81). When the wings are at the stern, the net may be fleeted aboard in the usual manner for vessels working over the stern, with the use of falls from the overhead boom (see Fig. 82). An alternative is to use a power block sited at the boom end with the boom lowered to allow the net to be worked at a convenient height.

In this operation, the cod-end is brought in either alongside, as shown in Figure 82, or over the stern and the fish dumped into the deck pounds on the after deck.

Fig. 78. Handling net aboard seine net vessel with after house.

Top: the net stacked on platform at stern of vessel, ready for setting. This vessel has an after house arrangement.

Bottom: the cod end is lifted aboard by falls from after boom. Fish are emptied into pounds between wheelhouse and rail.

Crew

A minimum of four crew on deck and one in the wheelhouse is necessary if a power block is used and at least two more if the net is brought aboard by hand. The total crew needed may exceed this

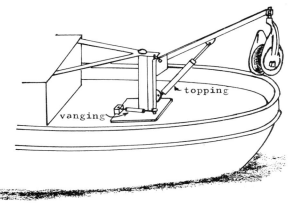

Fig. 80. One arrangement of power block on seine net vessel. In this arrangement, for a vessel with after house, the block is mounted at end of short boom stayed to the deckhouse. Hydraulic rams are used for topping and vanging.

depending on the amount of processing carried out aboard.

Tow Dragging (Japanese)

When fly dragging, the closing of the warps and net is achieved by a combination of towing and hauling in the warps, and while heaving up the vessel may well be moving astern.

The method used in Japan involves closing the warps and net entirely by towing, heaving up being delayed until the net is closed. In other respects the operation is very similar to fly dragging, but larger vessels of 100 feet L.O.A. or more are involved.

These vessels are often similar to stern ramp trawlers; they often utilize a ramp and large drums on which the warps are wound for storage, rather than their being laid out in coils. A typical arrangement is that of Figure 83 which shows the hauling sequence. The two warp storage drums are placed each side of the ramp, as also are twin towing blocks. Winches placed each side of the working deck have both V sheaves for warp hauling and a standard drum for working the net.

The warps are set out over the stern, being arranged so that they run off each drum as necessary, and when the dhan has been retrieved are placed in the twin towing blocks aft (Fig. 83). They are then taken over the winch V sheaves and to the storage drums; heaving continues until the wings are at the stern, when the warps are released from the towing blocks and placed in the stern ramp. Further heaving then pulls them up the ramp on to the working deck. With the wings aboard, the body of the net is

brought aboard in successive pulls using a line from the main winch barrels taken round a sheave at the forward end of the working deck, in a similar manner to net hauling board a stern ramp trawler. When the net is aboard, the cod-end is lifted by falls and emptied. The net may now be laid out in the stern ready for the next set, and the correct rigging of warps arranged.

Fig. 81. Arrangement of seine net vessel with wheelhouse forward.

Top: the winch (in this case hydraulic) is sited abaft wheelhouse with coiler just forward. Warp coils are stowed each side abreast house. Warps have clear run from winch barrels to stern.

Bottom: while towing and hauling, warps are lead from towing block at stern directly to winch drums. Deck is clear.

Anchor Dragging (Danish Seining)

The method evolved in Denmark and is the original seine netting technique from which fly dragging was a later development. Basically, the operation is the same as that described previously except that the vessel is anchored while hauling, and the warps and net are closed entirely by the winch.

Operation

When beginning the set, instead of placing a freely floating dhan buoy as in fly dragging, the buoy is anchored. After the gear has been set out, the vessel picks up the buoy and secures to the anchor line. The complete hauling sequence and getting the catch aboard is carried out at anchor.

Following the first set the vessel then fishes each sector in turn until it has covered all or part of the circular area of which the buoy and anchor are the centre (see Fig. 84).

This method of working is particularly effective on flatfish and requires a large area of seabed free from snags and rough patches.

Equipment

The equipment described here is that required for the smaller type of vessel particularly applicable to fly dragging and anchor dragging. Equipment used aboard the larger (Japanese) vessels has been noted briefly already.

Winches—either direct mechanical drive or hydraulic are applicable, the latter being a comparatively recent development. In either case it must be possible to obtain a number of hauling rates between 50 ft./min. and 300 ft./min. to suit the rates required at different stages of the operation. With mechanical drive, multi-speed gear boxes are usual, and in either case a coiler is geared to the barrel speed to gain correct coiling rates. The winch is a twin warping-barrel type, but is notable by the addition of a coiler, mounted as an integral part.

For net handling—power block mounted on boom or deck crane with slewing and topping arrangements. An alternative is to fleet the net by use of overhead falls and whip. For cod-end handling, a boom is necessary with falls and whip which can be taken to the winch barrels.

Fig. 82. Handling net aboard seine net vessel with wheelhouse aft.
Top: the net is brought aboard by fleeting.
Bottom: cod end is brought aboard by a tackle from the boom. Fish are emptied into deck pounds.

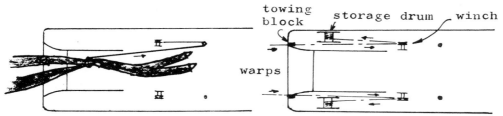

Fig. 83. Handling seine net with stern ramp. When towing, warps are run through blocks each side of ramp, and remain there throughout hauling until wings of net are at stern; warps are then removed from blocks and laid in ramp to be taken aboard. Warps are stowed on drums each side of ramp. Net is brought aboard by successive pulls using forward sheave and line from winch drum until cod end can be lifted and emptied in the usual manner.

Top left: warps are taken out of towing block and together hauled in to bring wings aboard.

Bottom left: net is brought aboard by successive pulls from winch drum taken round forward sheave.

Bottom right: when hauling, warps run from towing blocks, each side of ramp, are hauled by V-sheave and wound on storage drum.

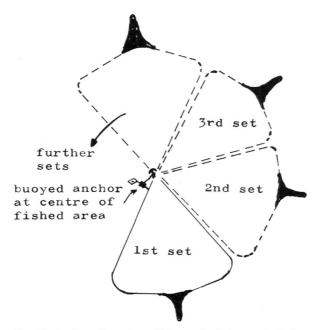

Fig. 84. Anchor Dragging. This method is particularly applicable where large areas of good bottom, free from snags and rough spots, are found. Following the first set from the anchor position, further sets are made to cover a circular area for which the anchor is centre.

Section 3

Static Gear

WHEREAS the fishing methods discussed previously have been "active", i.e., the vessel works the gear in order to capture fish, the effectiveness of static methods depends on the fish moving to the gear which is set out in a particular manner by the vessel and left for a period of time in one place; the vessel will return later to retrieve the gear and take aboard the catch.

The most common methods under this heading are:

1. Gillnets and traps.
2. Longlines.
3. Pots.

There are many methods of constructing and working these types of gear, depending on the traditional arrangements evolved to suit particular fishing areas, so that it is possible only to describe some of the more common techniques.

GILLNETS AND TRAPS

The gillnet is a large wall of netting which may be set either just above the sea bed when fishing for demersal species, or anywhere from mid-water to the surface when pelagic fish are being sought.

When working inshore in relatively shallow water, the nets are usually set and anchored in position, but an alternative is the drift net which is free to move according to tide and wind conditions.

The Gear

The net may consist of one sheet of twine in which the fish are trapped by their gills as they try to swim through, or several sheets of various mesh sizes in which they become entangled (tangle nets). The rigging of the gear varies widely, but two common arrangements for set gillnets are illustrated in Figure 85.

The top of the net is seized to a float or corkline and the bottom to a leadline. The combined action of the floats and weights maintains the vertical stretch of the net.

With bottom gillnets, sufficient weight is used to keep the leadline on the sea bed, while the buoyancy provided by the floats is sufficient only to maintain the vertical stretch. In the case of a mid-water gillnet on the other hand, sufficient floats are used to overcome the weight of the leadline which is used to maintain the stretch.

Lines from corkline and leadline at each end of the net are connected to lines running from anchors at the sea bed to surface buoys which show the location and extent of the gear and are used in hauling.

Several gillnets, each several hundred feet in length, may be set end to end in "fleets", and rather than being set in a straight line may be placed in hooked or curved formations. Usually, however, this is only possible in waters subject to little, if any tidal movement.

When drift netting, a typical arrangement is illustrated in Figure 85; usually a large number of nets will be set end to end, extending perhaps for several miles. At the free end of the fleet the net will be secured to a dhan buoy; further floats are secured at intervals along the line of set. At the far end, to leeward, the operating vessel secures to the net and drifts under wind action, so ensuring the net remains deployed correctly.

Vessels

Vessels of almost any size can undertake gill-netting or drift netting; the number of nets fished

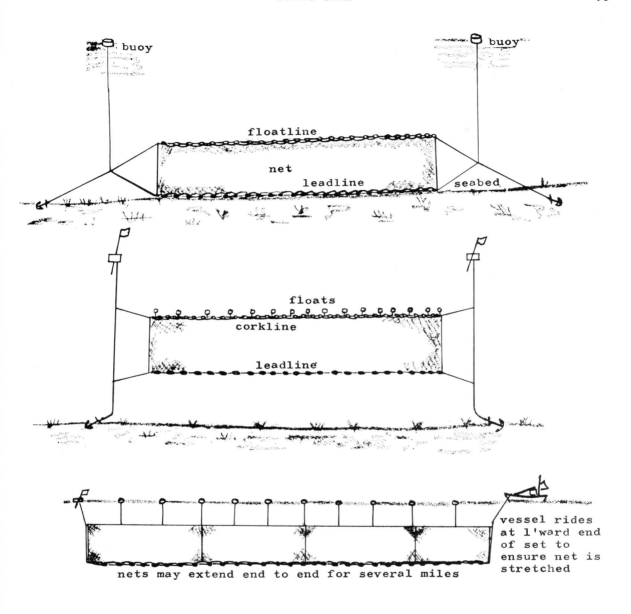

Fig. 85. Various methods of setting gillnets.
Top: bottom gillnet.
Middle: mid-water gillnet.
Bottom: drift net; surface gillnet.

being adjusted to suit the size of the operating vessel. An L.O.A. between 35 and 70 feet is common. An arrangement with wheelhouse and engine room forward or aft may be used, depending on the operating method adopted.

Operation

Two common operating techniques are:
1. Net set over stern, hauled over side.
2. Net set and hauled over stern.

Net set over stern, hauled over side. A typical layout for vessels using this method is shown in Figure 86. The net is set over a transom roller, and hauled by a gurdy mounted to starboard just forward of amidships. If the wheelhouse and engine room forward layout is used, the house is often extended aft over the hauling position to provide shelter for the deck crew. Alternatively an engine room and wheelhouse aft arrangement may be used, in which case sufficient deck space must be available abaft the

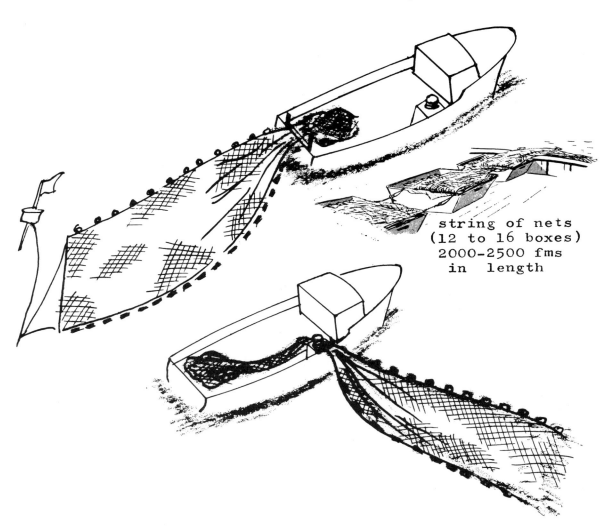

string of nets
(12 to 16 boxes)
2000-2500 fms
in length

Fig. 86. Gillnetting. Vessels with wheelhouse and engine room either forward or aft utilise this method. It is important that hauling gurdy is positioned sufficiently far forward that the pull allows the vessel to lie comfortably while hauling.
Top: setting: net is stacked inside transom or run out from individual net boxes.
Bottom: hauling: is by gurdy placed forward, usually to starboard, net is brought in over rail roller and fish shaken into deck pounds.

house for storing and handling the net. The width of the house must allow room for the net to be passed aft along the side deck when hauling so that it may be flaked down for the following set.

The forward house arrangement affords considerably greater protection to the deck crew than does the aft house layout; in the latter case, it is usual to fit a forecastle or whaleback, with the gurdy mounted abaft it, to increase crew protection.

When ready to set, with the net stacked in the stern or laid out in individual net boxes, the first anchor and dhan are placed overboard followed by the free end of the net; the vessel then moves slowly along the desired setting course, the net running out over the stern roller until the final anchor and dhan are laid. Several nets may be set out to form a suitable pattern, or they may be placed end to end in which case an anchor and dhan may be placed between groups. The operating vessel may remain in attendance at the grounds, or leave the area to return when it is desired to haul the gear.

When ready to haul, the vessel approaches the leeward end of the gear and retrieves the dhan and anchor line together with the net. The twine is placed around the gurdy and hauling commences, the net being guided to the gurdy by a rail roller with end guides. As the net is brought aboard, the gilled fish are shaken or taken from the net into deck pounds and the net is passed astern and flaked down ready for setting.

An alternative means of hauling is by a davit mounted power block sited so that the block extends outside the rail (see Fig. 87).

While hauling, the vessel is lying to the gear and sea, and moves gradually to windward as the net is taken aboard; it is important therefore that the gurdy is positioned so that the vessel may lie easily shoulder-to-sea while working.

Net set and hauled over stern. One method here provides for a very similar operating technique to that described previously, and appears very suitable for the wheelhouse forward arrangement.

The gear is set out over the stern as before, but is hauled from the stern by a davit mounted or boom mounted power block; while hauling the vessel is maintained stern-to (see Fig. 87).

Another vessel arrangement and operating technique on the west coast of North America is illustrated in Figures 88, 89 and 90. The fishing arrangement, applicable to any design with a forward house arrangement, is marked by the large net reel set in a well aft; a powered stern roller is

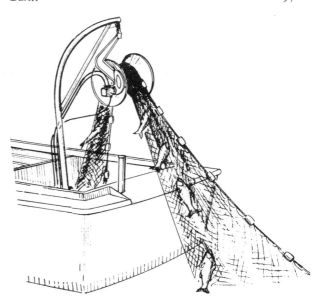

Fig. 87. Hauling gillnet by power block. Vessel hauls from leeward, stern-to. Alternatively, block may be mounted at boom tip lowered to required position.

usual with this method. While aboard, the net is stored on the reel, and when setting it is run off the reel over a transom roller into the water, to be set in the usual manner. When hauling, the vessel lies stern-to-weather; the net is passed over the powered roller to the drum, and these together carry out the hauling operation, the fish being taken from the net between the roller and drum.

In conditions where the vessel cannot work safely while lying stern to the weather, hauling may start from windward, the craft being kept under sufficient power to maintain this attitude while being drawn slowly astern as the net is taken in.

Equipment

This will depend very much upon the chosen operating method.

Side working. For setting, a net platform inside the transom is necessary on which the nets are stacked for setting, or some provision for siting net boxes. A free-running roller with end guides, some 30 to 40 inches in width should be sited at the transom. For hauling, either (a) a free-running roller or powered roller at the rail, some 30 inches in width with end guides, or a free-running sheave mounted outside the rail, leading the net to a powered gurdy. This gurdy may be mechanically driven from the

Fig. 88. High speed gillnetter. This type is common to the west coast of North America. The vessels are noteworthy for their light construction (often of aluminium) and high speed, both uncommon properties of commercial vessels. Note the powered net roller at the transom.

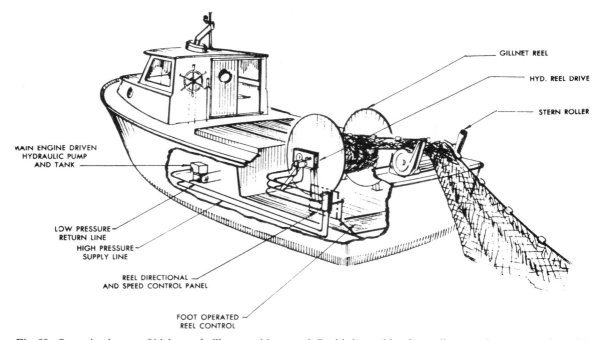

Fig. 89. Operating layout of high speed gillnetter with net reel. Reel is located in after well to permit easy operation with a single crew member. These reels are usually driven hydraulically, and are used in conjunction with a powered stern roller.

main engine or be hydraulic; or (b) a power block, davit or boom mounted above the rail.

Stern working. Either (a) for setting, a free-running system from stacked net or boxes over transom roller may be used. For hauling, a davit or boom mounted power block above the transom is required; or (b) for setting and hauling, a net reel and free-running or powered roller may be used. The reel size depends on the number of nets operated, but typically may be some 3 feet in diameter by 3 to 5 feet in length. The roller should have end guides and be some 30 inches in width.

Traps

This method is often used in areas through which fish regularly move or congregate. Traps may be of many sizes and configurations, but as the name implies rely for their effectiveness on preventing fish from leaving once they have been induced to enter.

Usually, the traps are set in relatively shallow water adjacent to the land, and extend from the surface to the bottom, at least at the mouth. Some traps have a bottom of netting over their whole area, while others have only a net base in the pocket area, relying mainly on contact with the sides and the sea bed to guide the fish and prevent their escape.

Figure 91 shows typical traps used on the east coast of the United States and the British Isles. The fish, on meeting the lead net, tend to follow the twine and so be guided into the mouth to pass into the heart or pockets where they are contained in a relatively small area. The operating vessel usually pays daily visits to the trap and "dries up" the pocket by hauling the webbing on board so that the catch may be brailed, or may heave the remaining part of the pocket aboard to dump the catch.

Vessel

Almost any vessel can set and attend a trap, but it is a particularly suitable method for relatively small craft from some 25 feet in length; the size ranges up to some 70 feet, however, especially if trap fishing is combined with another method, as is often the case.

Either a wheelhouse forward or house aft layout may be used, and the principal requirements for hauling are a gurdy or power block for drying up the net, combined in many cases with an overhead falls and whip arrangement. Figure 92 shows the arrangement of a 36-foot vessel designed to work traps around the Newfoundland coast. Engine power requirements are minimal, dependent on the free-running capability needed.

Fig. 90. Stern hauling gillnetter working with the aid of a powered net roller at transom.

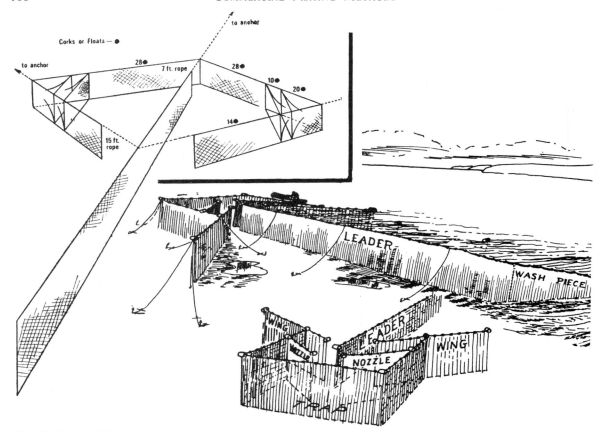

Fig. 91. Typical fish traps. Many variations in design are found from country to country and area to area, depending on local traditions and needs.
Top: Northumberland and Salmon "T" net, as used in the British Isles.
Bottom: design of trap common to the New England area of the U.S.A. The floating trap is constructed to fish from surface to bottom, and is therefore built to suit its location. The trap is held in position by a series of anchors and buoys; the leader net is often made fast to a ring bolt ashore. The wash piece is portable, being used only when certain species are running which tend to hug the shore.

LONGLINES

Longlining may be applied to the capture of demersal or pelagic fish, the gear being rigged to suit the species being sought and the area being fished; it is of particular importance in harvesting high individual value fish such as swordfish and halibut, but is widely used also for other species such as cod.

The basic method involves setting out a long length of line, often several miles, to which short lengths of line carrying baited hooks are attached every two to six feet. The fish are attracted by the bait, hooked, and held by the mouth until they are brought aboard the operating vessel which periodically hauls the gear.

The Gear

Typical arrangements of the gear for bottom longlining, and sub-surface or pelagic longlining are shown in Figure 93. There are wide variations in the dimensions, rigging and operation of the gear depending on the area, species and local tradition, so that it is possible only to describe common arrangements and techniques.

The Sub-Surface Longline

With this arrangement, the longline is maintained at its desired depth below the surface by regularly spaced lines running up to surface buoys which carry marker flags; these mark the set and are of assistance in the hauling operation.

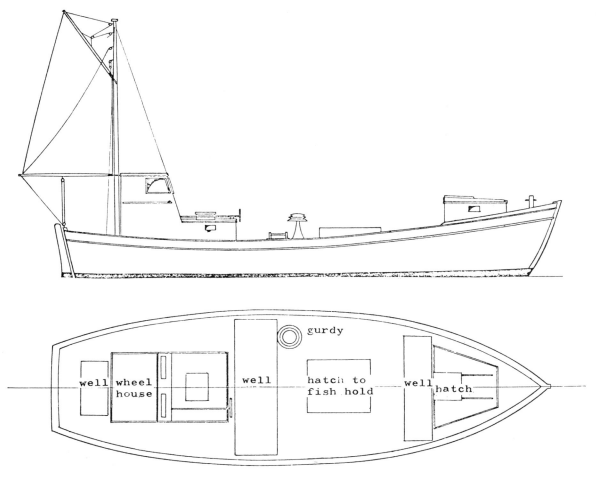

Fig. 92. Layout of 36-foot trap vessel. This vessel is designed to work the Newfoundland Coast. A diesel engine of 30 to 50 h.p. is fitted, together with a mechanically driven gurdy to haul the trap webbing.

The Bottom Longline

The longline, with its baited hooks, lies on or near the bottom and is maintained in position by anchors at each end. The anchors are buoyed at the surface and have marker buoys to show the location of the set, and to aid retrieval by the operating vessel. The lengths of line carrying the baited hooks may be spliced into the main set line at their required intervals as shown in Figure 98a. Alternatively, the baited lengths of line (ganglines or gangings) may be attached to the set line by snap-on connectors at stoppers (see Fig. 98b).

The line and hooks vary in size depending on the species being sought; the main set line may be rope or wire, and the gangings may vary from light rope to chain.

Vessels

The method is suitable for almost any size or type of vessel that can operate in the area being worked. Craft from twenty feet to well over a hundred feet in length are in regular use. It is possible to utilize almost any layout providing a relatively small area is available aft for setting operations.

Equipment and layout will be discussed as the various operating techniques are considered.

Operation

In all cases, longlines are set over the stern, but they may be hauled either from the stern or over the side rail.

Stern setting, side hauling. This operation is illustrated in Figures 94, 95, 96, 98. In the case of vessels having a forward house layout, a line hauler or gurdy is mounted at one rail immediately abaft the

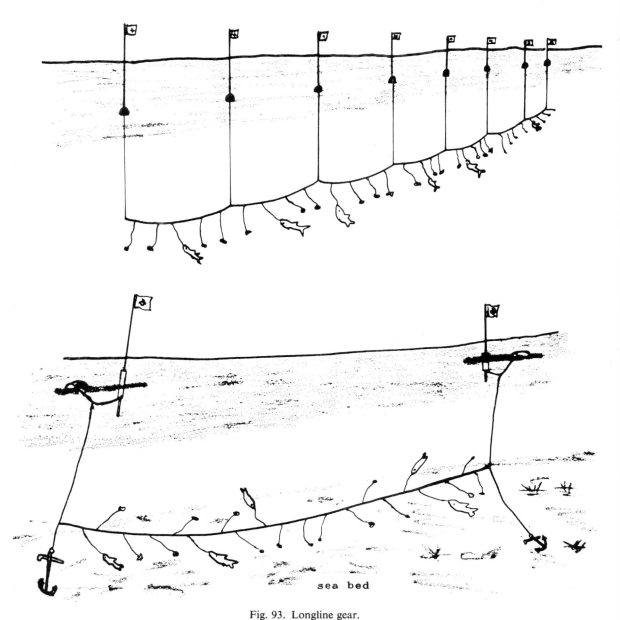

Fig. 93. Longline gear.
Top: sub-surface longline set: the line is suspended the required distance below the surface by regularly spaced buoys.
Bottom: bottom longline: the groundline runs along the sea bed and is maintained in position by anchors which are buoyed and marked to show location and extent of set.

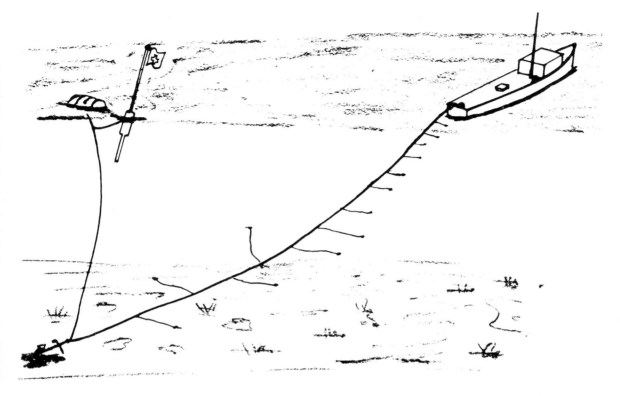

Fig. 94. Setting longline. Setting over stern: the vessel puts buoys, anchor line and end of groundline overboard, then steams along track paying out groundline.

house; the position of the hauler is important as it must permit the vessel to lie easily to the weather while hauling, and must therefore be somewhat forward of amidships. Figures 95 and 98 illustrate this. The hauling sheave of the gurdy may be mounted horizontally as in Figure 98a, or vertically as in Figure 100, and the small pulley is used to ensure an even pull is maintained. A double roller arrangement is sited at the rail (Fig. 98) to guide the line to the hauler. In vessels having an after house, the hauler is mounted forward, often in the shelter of a forecastle or whaleback.

A general view of the setting operation is shown in Figure 94 for a bottom longline. The procedure for subsurface gear is very similar, except that instead of anchors being involved, marker buoys attached to the line are put over at intervals.

To begin the set, the first anchor is put overboard with its line and buoys and one end of the longline (Fig. 99). The vessel then steams along the desired

track, while the longline runs out over the stern, slows and stops to place the final anchor and buoy arrangement.

The line and hooks may be prepared for setting either from a tub (Fig. 99) or a coil, if the hooked ganglines are permanently spliced to the groundline. With the coil arrangement the groundline is coiled with the baited hooks in the centre; if a tub is used, the line is loosely coiled in the tub with the baited hooks hung around the rim. A number of coils or tubs will usually be set out in series. In these cases the longline is set over a chute at the vessel's stern which may vary in construction, two typical designs being shown in Figure 96.

If snap-on ganglines are used, the groundline may be run off a spool, or from coils, the baited ganglines being set out in boxes and clipped to the stoppers as the line is run out (see Fig. 98b). Rather than the chute, the line may be set through rollers, the ganglines being snapped on just abaft the rollers.

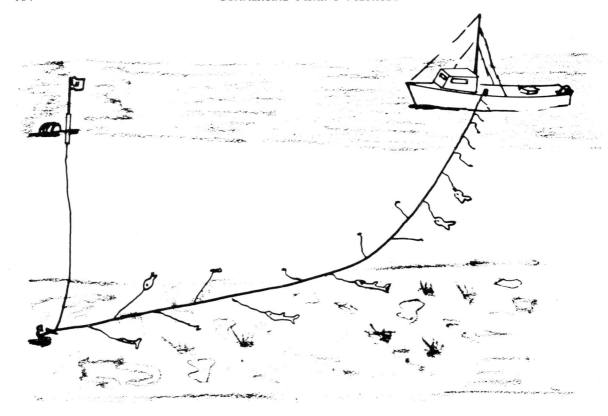

Fig. 95. Side hauling longline. A gurdy or other line hauler is used, the groundline running through roller guide at the rail. Vessel lies to the gear, hauling from leeward, so that correct positioning of hauler is important to ensure vessel lies comfortably to weather.

When the gear has been set, the operating vessel may remain in attendance, or steam away to return and retrieve the gear after an interval. In some cases hauling may commence almost immediately after the setting operation has been completed.

When ready to haul the gear, the vessel approaches the leeward end of the set and retrieves the marker buoy, anchor buoy and end of groundline in the case of a bottom longline, or the first marker buoy in the case of a sub-surface set. The groundline is then passed through the rail rollers, over the gurdy sheave, and hauling commences (see Figs. 95, 98).

As the hooked fish come to the rail, they are gaffed and placed in deck pounds. If snap-on ganglines are used, they are removed from the groundline before the line is wound on the spool or coiled ready for setting. The ganglines are placed in the box ready for setting, once the fish have been removed and placed in the deck pound. With permanently spliced lines, the groundline is coiled down ready for baiting. With the sub-surface long line, the buoys are brought aboard, disconnected from the groundline, and placed in racks as hauling proceeds.

Before the gear can be set again, the hooks must be baited and the prepared ganglines set out in boxes, or the lines coiled or tubbed.

Stern setting and hauling. This technique is normally applicable to vessels having a forward house layout.

In some cases, the operation may be similar to that described previously, except that the gurdy or spool is placed aft and hauling takes place over the stern. The vessel may haul from the leeward end of the set in good conditions, but if this is impracticable

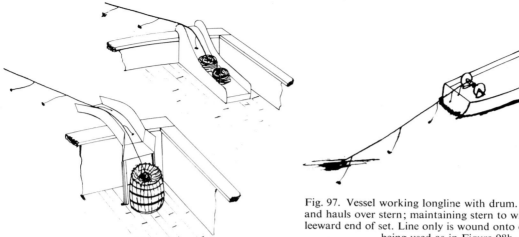

Fig. 97. Vessel working longline with drum. The vessel sets and hauls over stern; maintaining stern to wind, hauls from leeward end of set. Line only is wound onto drum, gangings being used as in Figure 98b.

Fig. 96. Setting longlines by chute.
Top: from coil: coils of baited up longline are laid at base of shute. Groundline is coiled with hooks at centre of coil.
Bottom: from tub: groundline is coiled in tub with baited hooks set around the tub rim so that they fly off as line runs out through chute.

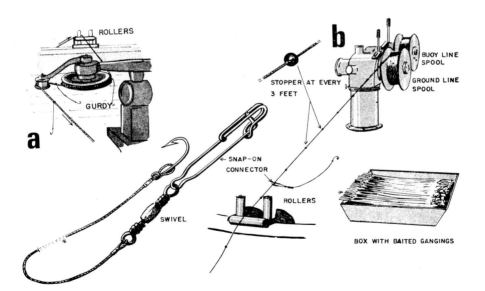

Fig. 98. Hauling gear for longline. (*from* N.M.F.S. circular 48 Fishing Vessels and Gear)
(a) Gurdy with horizontal sheave. Used with spliced gear.
(b) Operation of snap-on gear. The connector snaps onto groundline at regularly spaced stoppers. Baited gangings are set out in box ready for setting.

hauling may be started from windward, sufficient power being applied to maintain head to weather, the craft moving slowly down to leeward as the line is taken aboard.

An alternative technique may make use of a net reel or drum at the stern, as illustrated in Figure 97; vessels using such equipment are usually of a combination type in which the drum is used also for other methods and fisheries.

The groundline only is stored on the drum, which is used to set and haul the gear over the usual double fairlead at the transom, the snap-on type of gangline being used.

Equipment

For setting—a chute is necessary if spliced gang-lines are used; design may vary but should take the

Fig. 100. 85-foot longliner. Looking forward along working deck. This vessel uses sub-surface gear; the hauler may be seen at the starboard side, buoys are stowed in conveniently located racks.

Fig. 99. One method of baiting up and setting a bottom longline.

Top: baiting up a longline gear with sea clams.

Bottom: starting the set: the anchor has been dropped with one end of the line. The buoy marks the location. At the end of the set another buoy, anchor and flag are dropped.

general form of those shown in Figure 96. May also be used with snap-on ganglines. Alternatives are a spool and rollers or chute, suitable for use with snap-on type of ganglines, or a reel that is suitable only for use with snap-on gear.

For hauling—a gurdy with vertical or horizontal sheave and auxiliary pulley to maintain constant strain is suitable for use with spliced gear; a spool or reel is suitable for snap-on gear. The hauler or gurdy may be mechanically or hydraulically driven. Operating controls should be at the equipment. It is also possible to utilize the warping head of a trawl or purse winch for the hauling operation.

Other requirements—Buoy racks to hold marker buoys are especially important in the case of sub-surface gear where a large number of buoys are used; racks should be placed at vessel's side (see Fig. 100). Bait stowage arrangements may range from tubs in which cut bait is stowed aboard small vessels working daily, to live bait wells or a refrigerated holding room aboard large vessels spending considerable periods at sea. Crew shelter may be necessary to protect crew while baiting-up and/or hauling; these take the form of a large canopy (Fig. 101), an extension of the house, or in some of the latest vessels, a complete shelter deck.

Fig. 101. Crew Protection Arrangements.
Top: A longliner having removable canopy providing crew shelter aft while baiting up and setting. The hauler will be just abaft the deckhouse which protects crew while hauling.
Bottom: Norwegian full shelterdeck longliner, the 87-foot *Geir Peder*. The hauling winch is located at the hatch in the side forward, so providing complete crew protection. The chute for setting will be sited at a similar hatch aft to provide protection while baiting-up and setting.

POTS

This method is particularly applicable to the capture of crustaceans, such as lobster and crab, whose principal movement is by legs on the sea bed.

Pots of many differing sizes and configurations are set out and attract the species being fished by means of bait, either cut up fish or other sea ceatures, or in a prepared packaged form. The trap is constructed so that once the animal has entered through a specially designed entrance, it is unable to exit again and becomes trapped; it is then removed when the operating vessel retrieves the pot.

Pot fishing may be divided into two general classifications: inshore potting which is carried out by small vessels in depths of up to perhaps 50 fathoms, and deep sea potting which involves much larger vessels together with heavier pots and equipment.

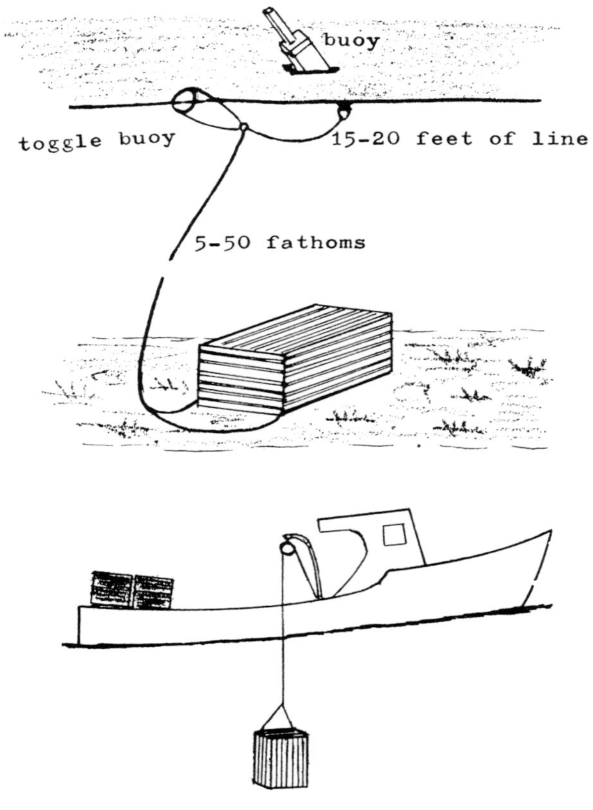

(a) Inshore Potting

Pots may be constructed of wood, plastic coated steel mesh or plastic mesh and may vary in shape between rectangular, semi-circular or circular cross section depending on the local custom, construction material, and the species being fished. Typical shapes are shown in Figs. 102 and 103. The entrance is usually at one end or at the top, and formed as a funnel of knitted webbing. Weight, often concrete is required to keep the trap on the sea bed and the correct way up. A rope line runs from the trap to surface buoys which may be of plastic, cork or wood.

Vessels

Vessels using both forward and after house arrangements are common in inshore potting operations; the type used appears to depend largely on local custom and development. Suitable arrangements for these layouts are shown in Figs. 103 and 104. It is important that a large amount of open deck space be arranged for pot stowage.

The length of vessels used varies from 25 to 45 feet.

Two common methods of hauling pots are illustrated in Figures 102 and 103. When the pots are being worked from the after deck, a hauler is mounted at the ship's side and hauls the pot line over a sheave which is either hung from a davit or from the wheelhouse structure. This hauler may be mechanically or hydraulically driven, the latter usually providing greater flexibility.

When pots are hauled using a vessel with wheelhouse aft, the operation is carried out well forward as shown in Fig. 103. Here a capstan arrangement is used, the line and pots being brought in over a rail roller.

Operation

When proceeding to the fishing grounds the lobster pots are stacked two or three deep over the working deck, often 60 to 100 being carried in this manner. If not already baited up, this is done on the way to the grounds. The pots may be set singly, each having its own surface line and buoy, or in "trots" or "trawls" where the traps are linked together by lines, surface lines and buoys being placed at intervals or at the first and last pots.

When at the desired location, the surface buoys

Fig. 102. Inshore potting operation.
Top: The pot is weighted to settle correctly on bottom and connected to surface buoys by line.
Bottom: vessel retrieves pot by hauling line over V-sheave pot hauler hung outboard on davit. Pot hauler may be mechanically or hydraulically driven. An alternative arrangement is to support hauler on framework hung from cabin side.

and line for the first pot are put overboard followed by the first pot; if a trot is being set, the vessel then steams slowly along the desired track paying out the connecting lines and placing successive pots. If the pots are being set singly, then the vessel places each in its desired position. The pots are left in position for a time which may vary from a number of hours to several days.

When the time comes to haul back, the vessel brings aboard the surface buoys, passes the line over the hauler or capstan and lifts the pot to the ship's side where it is laid on the rail or deck, the catch removed, rebaited if necessary, and set once more. This is continued for each pot if individual pot settings are used.

If a trot is being worked, the vessel retrieves the

Fig. 103. Pot fishing using after house and forward capstan.
Top: 35-foot double-ended vessel used in the British Isles pot fisheries. The hauler is sited forward.
Bottom: round pots constructed of wood and twine may be used. Approximately forty traps are set to a trawl which is anchored and buoyed at each end.

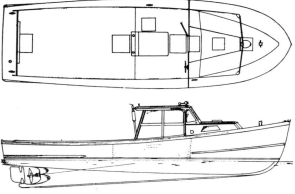

Fig. 104. Inshore potting vessel.
Left: vessel at work. Note the davit and pots on the rail.
Above: layout of typical inshore vessel 35 feet in length.

Fig. 105. Bringing aboard a king crab pot in Alaskan waters. A hydraulic V-groove hauler is hung at end of boom.
Boom is "active", i.e. has hydraulic vanging and topping arrangements. Pots weigh up to a ton when loaded.

Fig. 106. Typical davit mounted pot hauling arrangement found aboard many vessels working in the Alaskan king crab fishery. The davit is mounted immediately abaft the forecastle, and the hauler is driven hydraulically.

first pot as before, but continues hauling the connecting lines; each pot being handled in turn and reset, the vessel gradually moving along the line from leeward.

(b) Offshore Pot Fishing

This is a comparatively recent development in many areas, and is principally concerned with the harvesting of crustaceans on, and at the edge of, the continental shelves in depths of up to 300 fathoms.

The method of operation is very similar to inshore potting, except that much larger vessels and heavier equipment are utilized. Figures 105, 108, 109 illustrate the type of pot used; a typical pot might have a steel frame with steel or twine netting, measuring perhaps 7 feet by 7 feet by $2\frac{1}{2}$ feet with a

weight of 250 pounds when empty. When full, such a pot might hold a ton of lobsters or crabs. Alternatively, wooden pots, considerably larger than those used inshore, often prove successful.

The gear is worked in a very similar manner to that inshore, the pots usually being set individually, with a line and buoys, or in a string along a straight line, one boat working up to 80 pots. Two 20-inch pneumatic buoys plus a small auxiliary buoy may be used at the surface; latest developments involve the use of traps with no permanent surface line, a buoy being released from the pot to take a line to the surface on command from the operating vessel. This latter technique obviates any carrying away of buoys and line, and hence loss of the pot, by other surface craft working the area.

Vessels

Vessels working offshore are of necessity, considerably larger than their inshore counterparts, anywhere from 50 to 100 feet in length being typical. Either the house forward or house aft arrangement may be used, providing a large amount of deck space is available for pot stowage. As usual, the house forward arrangement will normally provide greater protection and better working conditions.

Pot handling arrangements vary depending on the size, type and weight of pots. Where large, heavy wire pots are in use, hauling gear may consist of a pot hauler mounted on a boom (Fig. 105) or on a davit (Fig. 106). Alternatively, the hauling line may be run through a snatch block at the boom end or davit, the line being taken to a winch warping drum (Fig. 107). In the case of these heavy pots, provision must be made to handle them on deck, while being brought aboard and while stowing, and this may be achieved by use of a boom able to cover the entire deck space.

In the case of lighter wooden pots, some more mechanized handling systems such as that shown in Figure 109 have been developed.

Operation

If a boom mounted V sheave is used, when ready to haul, the boom is lowered and the line placed over the V sheave; throughout hauling the boom remains in the lowered position until the pot reaches the surface when a hook, fixed to a chain from the boom end, is attached to the pot frame and the pot lifted aboard by topping and swinging the boom. When the catch has been dumped on the deck through a hinged lid, the pot is re-baited and

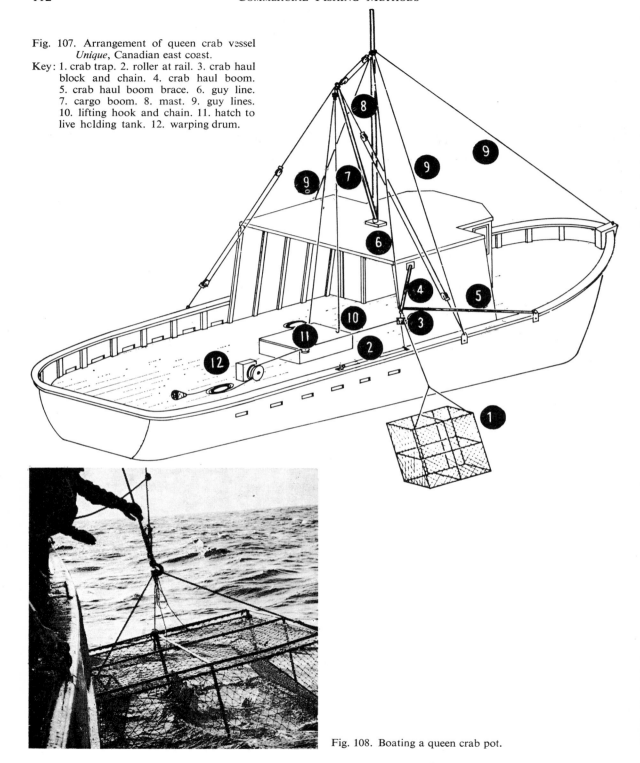

Fig. 107. Arrangement of queen crab vessel *Unique*, Canadian east coast.

Key: 1. crab trap. 2. roller at rail. 3. crab haul block and chain. 4. crab haul boom. 5. crab haul boom brace. 6. guy line. 7. cargo boom. 8. mast. 9. guy lines. 10. lifting hook and chain. 11. hatch to live holding tank. 12. warping drum.

Fig. 108. Boating a queen crab pot.

Fig. 109. 60-foot offshore pot vessel arranged for mechanized handling of large wooden pots.

Top left: aluminium track is arranged along starboard rail for rapid handling of pots. Moving pots on deck is facilitated by low angle fixed boom.

Top right: traps, which can be seen stacked on after deck, are set in strings of twenty to twenty five spaced about twenty fathoms apart. When hauling, the groundline is run through block on davit and taken to line hauler; crimps on the line provide an automatic stop for each trap. Pots come over the soft nose of the track and slide along for emptying and baiting. Rollers at forward and after end of track assist in pot handling.

Bottom: hydraulic pot hauler is sited abaft deckhouse and hydraulic winch mounted on boom. Drums at left hold groundline for sixteen to twenty strings of pots.

launched overboard, if fishing is to continue, or placed in its stowed position by manipulation of the boom. Some six to ten pots can be handled per hour in this manner.

If a davit mounted V sheave is used the pot is brought aboard by boom falls when at the ship's side.

On vessels using winch warping heads for hauling, a snatch block is hung from a davit; when ready to haul, the line is placed in the snatch block and taken to the warping head, the pot will be swung aboard by overhead falls as before.

Equipment

For hauling—all equipment should be hydraulically driven so that the line tension can be limited, preventing surging of the vessel from breaking the pot lines. All equipment should be controllable from the working position.

For pot handling aboard—boom with topping and swinging arrangements to permit placing of pot at extremities of working deck.

Bait stowage—due to the lengthy periods at sea involved in offshore work, frozen bait stowage will usually be necessary.

Other Mobile Gear

TROLLING

THIS method is particularly applicable to the capture of pelagic species having high individual value, and where high quality is necessary; typical examples are the salmon and tuna. Effectiveness depends on the fish schooling.

A number of lures or baited hooks are towed astern of a slowly moving vessel, the fish being hooked after snapping at the lure and held by the mouth until they can be brought aboard as the line is hauled in.

The Gear

Figures 110 and 111 show a typical gear arrangement for a troller. Several trolling lines, each having a number of lures on short leaders clipped to the main line, are towed from two or more outriggers arranged to hinge outboard from their vertically stowed positions. The storage, setting and retrieval of these lines, which are usually of piano wire, is handled by individual drums in a set of trolling gurdies. These may be placed abaft the house or between davits mounted each side of the vessel to support blocks for providing a satisfactory run of the trolling wires to the gurdy spools.

There are many methods in use for the towing and handling of the lines but two common arrangements are illustrated in Figures 110 and 111. In Figure 110, from the end of each outrigger, a length of chain or line (tag line) suspends a clip ring or similar device near the water level. The trolling wire runs from the gurdy drum or spool to a block hung from a davit at the ship's side aft, and hence through the clip ring and into the water. A number of lures or baited hooks, perhaps six to eight, are snapped to the line by connectors attached to two or three fathom leaders. The trolling lines are weighted by "cannonball" type sinkers which may weigh up to 50 pounds.

The lines are arranged to tow at different depths, so providing a spread of coverage, by varying the length run out and the weight.

An alternative arrangement is illustrated in Figure 111, where several lines are towed from the same outrigger. Blocks are suspended on springs at several positions along each outrigger pole; the towing line is taken from the gurdy spool, over a block at the davit, round the appropriate block on the outrigger, and streamed astern.

Vessels

Small vessels are typical of this method, usually being operated by a crew of one or two men; the gear arrangement is such that the helmsman can run the gurdy and handle the catch himself. Vessel lengths between 25 and 50 feet are common, normally with a wheelhouse forward arrangement, allowing a clear well or working deck aft.

Operation

The vessel steams at one or two knots through the fishing area, the hooking of a fish being denoted by a jerk at the outrigger. To retrieve the fish, the appropriate gurdy spool is actuated to wind in the trolling line.

When a tag line and clip arrangement is used, the trolling line is unclipped when the tag line clip reaches the rail, and empty leaders unclipped as hauling is continued until the gurdy is stopped when the hooked fish can be gaffed and brought aboard. The line is then run out again from the

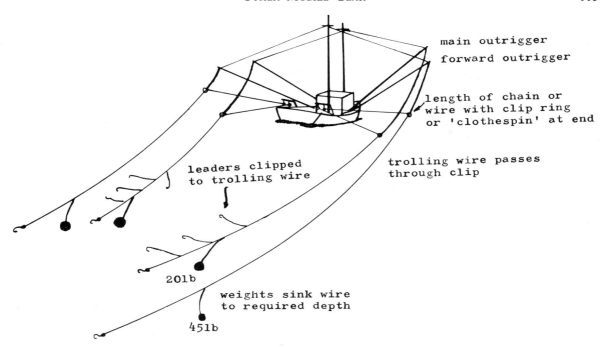

main outrigger

forward outrigger

length of chain or
wire with clip ring
or 'clothespin' at end

trolling wire passes
through clip

leaders clipped
to trolling wire

20lb

weights sink wire
to required depth

45lb

Fig. 110. Trolling operation. Typical operation using four outrigger poles and four lines; lines are of stainless steel 6-strand wire, approx. ⅛ inch diameter. Main poles are about the length of the boat, six inches diameter at their base, two inches diameter at the tip, and are connected to the deck by hinged plates. Forward poles are about two thirds the length of the main poles. When running, main poles are raised to seat in cross trees, forward poles may use this arrangement or may be held by a three-way guy rig. Leaders are between one and three fathoms length and are connected through two foot long rubber "stretchers" which clip to the main line. The main lines are taken from the gurdy spools over the davit sheave (see Fig. 112) and through a slip ring or "clothes pin" at the end of a rope or chain attached to the outrigger tips. Lead "canonball" weights at the ends of the lines are used to control fishing depth and keep lines apart; these weights are attached to the lines by leather "breaking straps" which are designed to break should the weight hang up on the sea bed, rather than carry away line and outrigger.

gurdy spool, the leaders being reattached and the tag line clipped on as it is paid out to the required scope for fishing.

If the lines are towed directly from outriggers, the gurdy is used to haul in the trolling line until the first leaders are in sight; the vessel is then turned so that the line can be reached from the stern, the fish gaffed and brought aboard, and the line run out once more with the vessel back on course.

Equipment

Outriggers should be light and reasonably flexible, wood poles being useful. A gooseneck arrangement at the foot is necessary to permit correct rigging outboard, and topping for stowage. Fore and aft guys and topping arrangements, which may be hand operated, are required and provision should be made for securing the poles vertically for stowing. Equipment on the outriggers will depend on the chosen gear arrangement. Light davits or other similar structure to support blocks should be mounted to provide suitable leads to the spools of the trolling gurdy. The trolling gurdy (see Fig. 112) should have separate spools for the wire of each trolling line, individually controlled. Hydraulic or mechanical drive may be used; the former providing greater flexibility.

HARPOONING

This method can be used commercially on large species having high individual value, such as the swordfish. Work and time involved in searching, capturing and bringing aboard each fish restricts the operation to such particularly valuable species.

Fig. 111. Modern 41-foot troller. Three wires are towed from each outrigger pole. With this rig, the wire is taken from the gurdy drum over the davit sheave and to a sheave suspended on springs at the required position on the outrigger; from here the wire passes into the water.

The Gear

Figure 113 illustrates swordfish harpooning gear; the harpoon is built from a wood pole having a steel shaft with double barb at its forward end. From the barb end of the pole, a "hunting" line, some 40 to 150 fathoms in length, is secured to a buoy which is often of the wooden keg type; this buoy shows the movement of the fish after it has been struck.

A retrieving line runs from the pole of the harpoon to the operating vessel; both the hunting and retrieving lines are run out from coils or tubs positioned on the vessel's foredeck.

Vessel

Vessels used for harpoon fishing are usually marked by the "stand" some 12 feet in length projecting forward of their bows (see Fig. 113), where the striker is positioned. A tub or crow's nest arrangement is often fitted on the mast for spotting.

Size is not of great importance, often being between 25 and 70 feet, but the vessel must have a reasonable speed, in the order of 10 knots, and be very manoeuvrable. Crew may be between two and four men.

Fig. 112. Set of trolling gurdies. Each trolling wire is wound on its individual spool. The spools are usually driven hydraulically and fitted with gearboxes to facilitate handling.

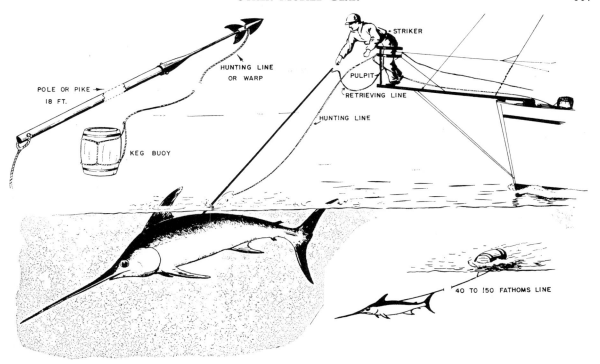

POLE OR PIKE → 18 FT.

HUNTING LINE OR WARP

STRIKER

PULPIT

RETRIEVING LINE

HUNTING LINE

KEG BUOY

40 TO 150 FATHOMS LINE

Fig. 113. Harpooning operation. Used for large species having high individual value, such as the swordfish, shown here. The harpoon is attached by line to a float, often a buoy of keg type, and to the operating vessel by a recovery or tag line. The movement of the fish, once struck, is shown by the buoy, so that the vessel may follow its movements. Method is suitable for both small and larger vessels, providing they are manoevrable. The striker positions himself on the stand extending forward of the bow and the line is run out from a keg or free running spool.

Operation

When a fish is sighted, the vessel is steered towards its position, and the striker positions himself on the stand with the harpoon made ready directing the helmsman so that he can make his strike and capture the fish.

On the harpoon taking hold, the fish is allowed to run, the hunting line and buoy going overboard to show the fish's movement and allow the vessel to follow. The retrieving line is also allowed to run out as necessary until it may be snubbed, and the fish tired out, so that the vessel can be brought to a halt alongside. In small vessels, the fish will be brought aboard by a whip using a sling around the tail and working over the side. In the case of larger vessels with too great a freeboard, a small boat is put overboard to place the sling and assist in handling.

Equipment

The stand should be twelve to sixteen feet in length, extending forward of the bow, with adequate lifelines and with a pulpit at its forward end. A barrel or pulpit arrangement should be sited at the cross trees or above for the spotter.

POLE AND LINE

Pole and line fishing is undertaken for pelagic fish which school, and is particularly applicable to such species as tuna or large mackerel type fish having reasonably high individual value.

A number of men, equipped with fishing poles, position themselves around the vessel and heave the fish aboard as they strike at the hooks.

Fig. 114. Pole Fishing. The men stand on a platform outside the bulwark, which may extend around the sides of the vessel. Either unbaited or baited hooks may be used, or lures. Each man uses a long heavy bamboo rod with a permanently attached line and hook. As fish strikes, the operator heaves and throws the fish forward onto the deck by rod action. A live bait tank may be sited at the centre line, or small bait boxes used.

Gear

The fishing gear consists of a bamboo pole, some twelve to fourteen feet in length, to which is attached a line having a feather or other lure with a barbless hook; alternatively, bait may be used. In some cases, two men using poles connected to a common line and hook may be required for large fish.

Vessels

The vessel is equipped with a platform outside, and lower than, the bulwarks around the stern; in some cases the platform extends forward along each side. Live or frozen bait is mainly used for "chumming" (attracting fish to feed by scattering bait fish) so that bait tanks or storage will be provided with individual bait positions for the fishermen.

The deck or a false deck will often be arranged to slope upwards to the transom so that fish when heaved aboard slide forward to a handling position at which they are cleaned before being placed below. The size of vessel depends principally on the area to be fished and may range from 45 feet upwards.

Operation

When a school is reached, the pole fishermen take their positions and begin "chumming" to bring the fish to a feeding frenzy. Each man casts his line astern as the vessel passes slowly through the school, the fish snap at the splash of the hook and upon one striking, the fisherman heaves on his pole to fling the fish behind him and on to the deck; as the hook is barbless, the fish is disengaged automatically as the line tightens, and slides forward along the sloping deck.

Equipment

A platform should be arranged around the stern, with protective rails, safety lines, and belts for individual fishermen. If bait is used, either refrigerated storage or live bait tanks are necessary. Individual bait boxes or lure storage is required.

Useful Additional Reading

1. Fishing Boats of the World I, edited by J. O. Traung. Fishing News (Books) Ltd. London.
2. Fishing Boats of the World II, edited by J. O. Traung. Fishing News (Books) Ltd. London.
3. Fishing Boats of the World III, edited by J. O. Traung. Fishing News (Books) Ltd. London.
4. Modern Fishing Gear of the World I, edited by H. Kristjonssen. Fishing News (Books) Ltd. London.
5. Modern Fishing Gear of the World II, edited by H. Kristjonssen. Fishing News (Books) Ltd. London.
6. Proceedings of F.A.O. Technical Conference on Fish Finding, Purse Seining and Aimed Trawling, Reykjavik, May 1970. In press. Modern Fishing Gear of the World III, edited by H. Kristjonssen. Fishing News (Books) Ltd. London.
7. Proceedings of Conference on Mechanization and Automation in the Fishing Industry, Montreal, Feb 1970. (Canadian Fisheries Report No. 15.)
8. Proceedings of Canadian Atlantic Offshore Fishing Vessel Conference, Montreal, Oct. 1966. (Canadian Fisheries Report No. 7.)
9. Various publications of Department of Fisheries of Canada, Ottawa.
10. Various publications of the U.S. National Marine Fisheries Service, Washington.
11. Various publications of the White Fish Authority, London.
12. The German One Boat Midwater Trawl. Reprint from series of articles in Fishing News International.
13. Two Boat Midwater Trawling for Herring. New England Marine Resources information program, Rhode Island, U.S.A.
14. Various booklets published by Bridport Gundry Ltd., Bridport, England.
15. Deep Sea Trawling and Wing Trawling, by John Garner. Gourock Ropework Co., Port Glasgow, Scotland.
16. Modern Deep Sea Trawling Gear, by John Garner. Fishing News (Books) Ltd. London.
17. How to Make and Set Nets, by John Garner. Fishing News (Books) Ltd. London.
18. The Seine Net, Its Origin, Evolution and Use, by David Thomson. Fishing News (Books) Ltd. London.